The Natural History of

MOLES

The Natural History of Mammals Series
Comstock Publishing Associates
a division of Cornell University Press

Published in the United Kingdom as
Christopher Helm Mammal Series
Edited by Dr. Ernest Neal, MBE, former President of the Mammal
Society

The Natural History of

MOLES

Martyn L. Gorman and R. David Stone

COMSTOCK PUBLISHING ASSOCIATES
A division of CORNELL UNIVERSITY PRESS
Ithaca, New York

FEB 1 8 1993

First published 1990 by Christopher Helm Ltd. and Cornell University Press

Line illustrations by Robert Donaldson and Bob Duthie

Library of Congress Cataloging-in-Publication Data

Gorman, M.L. (Martyn L.)
　The natural history of moles/Martyn L. Gorman, R. David Stone,
　　p.　cm.　(The Natural history of mammals series)
　Includes bibliographical references.
　ISBN 0–8014–2466–6 (alk. paper)
　1. Moles (Animals)　I. Stone, R. David.　II. Title.
QL737.I57G67　1990
599.3′3 — dc 20

Phototypeset by OPUS Oxford
Printed and bound in Great Britain by Hartnolls Ltd, Bodmin, Cornwall

Contents

To the little gentleman
in black velvet.

Colour plates

Figures

Tables

Acknowledgements

I would like to place on record my gratitude for the great deal of help that I have received throughout my studies of moles and during the production of this book. Sincere thanks, therefore to:

The Natural Environment Research Council and the University of Aberdeen for financial support.

Grampian Regional Council and John Malster for allowing ready access to study-sites in the beautiful surroundings of the Haddo House Country Park.

Robert Donaldson and Bob Duthie for doing such a very good job with the diagrams and illustrations.

Bob Ralph, proof-reader extraordinaire, for saving me from a number of very red faces.

Paul Racey, who first brought to my attention the fact that the mole is a very odorous creature and who thus set me off on the trail of research that was eventually to lead to this volume.

Last, but far from least, to all my colleagues and students at the University of Aberdeen, past and present, for providing such a convivial and stimulating environment in which to work. I hope that they all realise just how grateful I am. It is invidious to pick out anyone for special mention, but nevertheless, I would like to play tribute to my friend John Ollason for tending so very carefully the bright flame of scholarship.

Martyn Gorman
Aberdeen

Series editor's foreword

In recent years there has been a great upsurge of interest in wildlife and a deepening concern for nature conservation. For many there is a compelling urge to counterbalance some of the artificiality of present-day living with a more intimate involvement with the natural world. More people are coming to realise that we are all part of nature, not apart from it. There seems to be a greater desire to understand its complexities and appreciate its beauty.

This appreciation of wildlife and wild places has been greatly stimulated by the world-wide impact of natural-history television programmes. These have brought into our homes the sights and sounds both of our own countryside and of far-off places that arouse our interest and delight.

In parallel with this growth of interest there has been a great expansion of knowledge and, above all, understanding of the natural world — an understanding vital to any conservation measures that can be taken to safeguard it. More and more field workers have carried out painstaking studies of many species, analysing their intricate behaviour, relationships and the part they play in the general ecology of their habitats. To the time-honoured techniques of field observations and experimentation has been added the sophistication of radio-telemetry whereby individual animals can be followed, even in the dark and over long periods, and their activities recorded. Infra-red cameras and light-intensifying binoculars now add a new dimension to the study of nocturnal animals. Through such devices great advances have been made.

This series of volumes aims to bring this information together in an exciting and readable form so that all who are interested in wildlife may benefit from such a synthesis. Many of the titles in the series concern groups of related species such as otters, squirrels and rabbits so that readers from many parts of the world may learn about their own more familiar animals in a much wider context. Inevitably more emphasis will be given to particular species within a group as some have been more extensively studied than others. Authors too have their own special interests and experience and a text gains much in authority and vividness when there has been personal involvement.

Many natural history books have been published in recent years which have delighted the eye and fired the imagination. This is wholly good. But it is the intention of this series to take this a step further by exploring the subject in great depth and by making available the results of recent research. In this way it is hoped to satisfy to some extent at least the curiosity and desire to know more which is such an encouraging characteristic of the keen naturalist of today.

Ernest Neal
Bedford

1 Introduction

If we were to be transported 250 million years back in time it would be to a strange world dominated by reptiles; a world in which the members of that immensely successful group the dinosaurs were rapidly diversifying, destined eventually to fill a very wide range of niches indeed, from plant eaters to flesh eaters, from walkers to runners, from swimmers to flyers. The dinosaurs were not totally alone, however, for scampering about in the leaf litter, amongst their great feet, were small furry creatures whose descendants would, in the fullness of time, inherit the earth. These insignificant individuals were the first of the mammals, animals which had finally made the evolutionary transition from the reptilian grade. They were shrew-like beasts, the size of a modern mouse, presumably with small eyes and ears and equipped with a long pointed snout that bristled with sensory whiskers, and which was held in a state of constant agitation. From their diminutive size, and from the style of their dentition, we can be pretty certain that these creatures made their living by eating insects and other small invertebrates. Most importantly, they had the ability to maintain a constant body temperature over a wide range of ambient conditions, and in this they were aided by a dense covering of that most momentous of mammalian developments, fur.

Some writers have argued that it was this ability to regulate body temperature that allowed the early mammals to survive in the shadow of those terrible lizards. By staying warm, so the argument goes, they were able to be active at night, at a time when their cold-blooded reptilian predators and competitors had become sluggish and inactive. Unfortunately such an argument does not stand too close a scrutiny since it is a matter of debate as to whether the dinosaurs were, in fact, cold-blooded. Even if they were, the larger ones at least would have retained enough of the sun's heat to remain active at night, like an electric night-storage heater in reverse. A further nail in the coffin of this line of argument is the fact that many modern, and definitely cold-blooded, insectivorous lizards are active by night.

By whatever means, the fact remains that the early mammals did of course survive and eventually triumph. For many millions of years, however, they were able to do little but hang on, changing little in the process. Having been so effectively pre-empted by the extensive adaptive

1

Figure 1.1 Top: Pyrenean desman. Bottom: Russian desmans

radiation of the dinosaurs they were to endure 140 million years of evolutionary frustration. Their relief was to come quite suddenly, some 65 million years ago, with the rapid demise of the dinosaurs for reasons that are far from clear but which are currently hotly debated. With this change in their fortunes, the mammals were largely freed from

Figure 1.2 European mole in tunnel

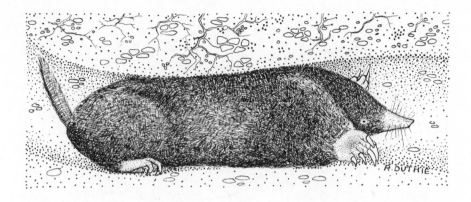

competitive pressure; their time had truly come! Nonetheless, biological change takes time, and for hundreds of thousands of years nothing too dramatic happened; the mammals remained small and shrew-like and continued to crunch their way through whatever invertebrate life they happened to bump into. In due course, however, the world was to see a glorious flowering of mammals as they embarked on their grand adaptive radiation. Within the next ten million years all of the existing mammalian orders became established, with body-forms as specialised and as varied as, for example, the great whales of the oceans and the bats of the air.

Not all mammals have changed so dramatically, and today there are still species around which have altered relatively little in the last 150 million years. These animals retain many of the features which were present in the earliest mammals. They are usually small, with long pointed snouts and are covered in short, close-set fur (Figures 1.1 and 1.2). Most walk in a plantigrade style, with their heels and toes both firmly on the ground, while their limbs are short and are usually equipped with a full complement of five digits. In many members of the group the genital and urinary systems share a common exit, while in the males the testes do not descend into a scrotum but instead are either abdominal, inguinal or held in a sac in front of the penis. The eyes and ears of these little mammals are relatively small and may be all but invisible. It is not surprising, therefore, to find that they rely to a great extent on their senses of touch and smell and that the areas of the brain which deal with such information are relatively well developed. In general, however, they have small brains which are smooth and without the wrinkles that serve to increase the surface area of the higher centres in more advanced mammals.

Most of them live in a simple social order, being solitary creatures, and are often active only by night. Usually they have retained their ancestral and ancient diet of invertebrates, particularly insects, which they tackle with a primitive and relatively full dentition (Figure 1.3). This usually consists of a continuous row of teeth and often comprises 3 incisors, 1

3

Figure 1.3 Skulls of European mole (a), Russian desman (b and c) and star-nosed mole (d) ventral view

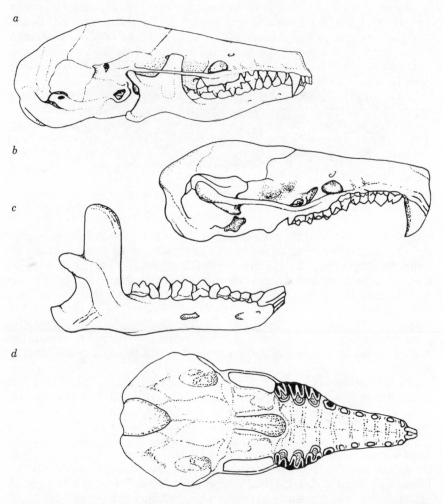

a

b

c

d

canine, 4 premolars and 3 molars in each half-jaw, a total of 44 teeth, the maximum dentition normally found in placental mammals. The crowns of the cheek teeth are characteristically equipped with W-shaped cusps that serve to assist in crushing the exoskeletons of insects and other invertebrates.

Detailed anatomical studies of these kinds of animals, particularly of their skulls and teeth, indicate very strongly that they are all descended from a common ancestor and therefore they are placed together in a single taxonomic grouping, the order Insectivora. This assemblage, which originated in the Cretaceous Period, about 135 million years ago, currently consists of around 345 species and is subdivided into six families; the Solenodontidae (solenodons), the Tenrecidae (tenrecs), the Chrysochloridae (golden moles), the Erinacidae (hedgehogs and moonrats — what a wonderful name!), the Talpidae (moles, shrew-moles and desmans), and the largest family of all, with 70 per cent of the species, the Soricidae (shrews). Three of the families, the hedgehogs, the shrews and the moles, are quite widespread in distribution with representatives in most parts of the world with the exception of Australia, much of South America, Greenland and Antarctica. The other three families are much more restricted; the solenodons to Hispaniola and Cuba, the tenrecs to Madagascar, the Seychelles and Equatorial West Africa, and the golden moles to sub-Saharan Africa.

We have been at some pains to stress that the insectivores retain a variety of characteristics which are regarded as being primitive. However, it is important to understand that we are nevertheless dealing with a group of very successful creatures, and that many species have evolved some highly advanced and specialised adaptations. Two examples will suffice to illustrate the point; one is to do with defence, the other

Figure 1.4 Distribution of the families Talpidae and Chrysochloridae

■ Talpidae   ▦ Chrysochloridae

Figure 1.5 The golden mole Amblysomus hottentotus

with attack. Faced with a variety of predatory animals, the fur of a number of hedgehogs and tenrecs has become modified to form batteries of protective spines. The solenodons and some of the shrews, in contrast, have gone on the offensive and have evolved specialised salivary glands that produced a poisonous secretion which allows them to tackle prey that would be far too large for an individual animal to kill by biting alone. In addition, these toxic secretions may also serve to weaken and paralyse the prey, so that it can be cached and then eaten at a later date.

It is among the members of the Talpidae and Chrysochloridae, however, that we find the most extreme modifications and specialisa-tions, usually for digging but in a few species for swimming. These are the animals which are to form the subject of this book.

The golden moles originated in Africa, probably from a tenrec-like ancestor, and they are known from as far back as the lower Miocene, some 25 million years ago. Despite their long history, they have never managed to expand beyond the confines of that continent, and today they occupy a range of relatively dry habitats south of the Sahara, stretching from Cameroon, Zaire, Uganda and Tanzania south to the Cape (Figure 1.4). All are solitary, burrowing animals with compact, streamlined bodies, short limbs and no external sign of a tail (Figure 1.5). Despite their common name, not all golden moles are golden in colour, although most do sparkle with lustrous sheens in a most spectacular way (Plate 1). *Chrysochloris asiatica*, for example, is dark brown with sheens of green, violet and purple depending upon the angle of the incident light. (One might well wonder why an animal that is restricted to southern Africa has been given the specific name *asiatica*. The blame lies firmly with the

Table 1.1 The family Chrysochloridae, golden moles

Chrysochloris

C. asiatica	Cape golden mole	W Cape Province
C. stuhlmanni	Stuhlmann's golden mole	E Africa

Eremitalpa

E. granti	Grant's golden mole	SW Africa

Calcochloris

C. obtusirostris	Yellow golden mole	S Africa

Cryptochloris

C. wintoni	De Winton's golden mole	W Cape Province
C. zyli	Van Zyl's golden mole	SW Cape Province

Amblysomus

A gunningi	Gunning's golden mole	Transvaal
A. hottentotus	Hottentot golden mole	S Africa
A. iris	Zulu golden mole	SE Africa
A. julianae	Juliana's golden mole	Transvaal

Chlorotalpa

C. arendsi	Arend's golden mole	E Zimbabwe
C. duthiae	Duthie's golden mole	S Cape Province
C. leucorhina	Congo golden mole	WC Africa
C. sclateri	Sclater's golden mole	S Africa
C. tytonis	Somali golden mole	Somalia

Chrysospalax

C.trevelyani	Giant golden mole	SE Cape Province
C. villosus	Rough-haired golden mole	SE Africa

great taxonomist Linnaeus, who mistakenly thought that the type specimen had originated in Siberia!) The fur, which is moisture-repellent, is backward set as in most other mammals, and overlies a dense underfur. All golden moles are blind, with vestigial eyes that remain closed from birth onwards and which later become covered with fur. The head is pointed to ease its passage through the soil and the muzzle is capped with a leathery patch that is used in digging. The necessary orifices of the body are relatively sand-proof; the ears, for example, are simple openings without pinnae and are covered with fur. The forelimbs each with four digits and equipped with stout, sharp claws, are strong and used in digging, while the rear limbs are of more normal dimensions.

Despite their long evolutionary history, golden moles appear to have changed little over geological time. Today, they are represented by about 17 species which are generally placed in seven genera (Table 1.1) and which, between them, occupy a variety of habitats including grassveld, forests, river banks, edges of swamps, mountains, deserts and lowveld scrub. It must be admitted, however, that the taxonomy of the group is

Figure 1.6 Swimming star-nosed moles

not well understood and that this classification must be regarded as provisional, particularly so at the generic level (Corbet & Hill, 1986).

The family Talpidae contains as queer a set of bedfellows as one could hope to meet; on the one side the moles and shrew-moles (Plates 3–6), which are more or less fossorial and, on the other, the desmans (Plate 7) which are semi-aquatic. The moles and desmans originated in Europe where their fossil record extends back some 45 million years into the late Eocene. Today they are spread throughout Europe, Asia and North America but are absent from Africa, where their niche is occupied by the golden moles. The fossil record in North America stretches back almost

8

as far as it does in Europe, with remains of moles having been found in rocks from the Oligocene. Nevertheless, not all the species are of such great antiquity, since recent taxonomic studies suggest that there have been numerous invasions from the Old World by talpids in the last 40 million years (Yates & Greenbaum, 1982).

In general, moles and desmans have elongated cylindrical bodies which terminate in a long, tubular and pig-like snout. The muzzle, which is relatively naked apart from a few sensory hairs, is highly mobile and extends well beyond the end of the upper jaw (see Figure 3.8, page 50). In the star-nosed mole of North America, the nose is uniquely divided at its end into a Medusa-like rosette of 22 naked, fleshy and mobile tentacles (Figure 1.6). The surface of this hydra, like the more conservative rhinaria of the other talpid species, is covered in a multitude of minute touch-sensitive projections known as Eimer's organs. Indeed, both moles and desmans live in a sensory world that is dominated by smell and, more particularly, by touch. The eyes are structurally complete but minute and hidden in the fur, although they are not usually covered by skin. There are no external ears in any of the species with the exception of the Asiatic shrew-moles.

Although moles and desmans have many anatomical features in common, they enjoy very different ways of life and it is not surprising that they are in some ways fundamentally different from each other. The desmans are highly adapted for swimming and in this they are aided by a long tail which is laterally flattened and fringed with stiff hairs, and which acts as a rudder. However, during swimming the major propulsive force is provided by the legs, which are heavily muscled and relatively long, with the back feet three times the length of the front, and longer than either the lower or upper part of the legs. The resistance of the toes and fingers against the water is increased by means of webbing and by fringes of stout hairs. Water, of course, tends to penetrate any orifice and to prevent this the nostrils and ears of desmans are equipped with watertight valves. Today, there are only two living species of desmans and both are placed in the subfamily Desmaninae: the Pyrenean desman *Galemys pyrenaicus*, which weighs around 65 g and the larger 500 g Russian desman *Desmana moschata*. Although desmans were apparently widely spread across Europe in pre-Pleistocene times they are now very restricted in distribution and becoming increasingly so. The Pyrenean desman occurs only in fast-flowing mountain streams on the northern half of the Iberian peninsula and on the French side of the Pyrenees (Richard, 1976). As one might guess from its name, the Russian desman is restricted to the rivers and lakes of European Russia, particularly the Don, Volga and lower Ural.

Whereas the desmans are adapted for easy passage through water, the moles have pulled out all the evolutionary stops to become efficient and powerful diggers. Of all the living insectivores, moles are probably most closely related to shrews and today the American and Asiatic shrew-moles follow a way of life that is in some ways intermediate between the two. Whereas the more specialised moles dig tunnels and obtain most of their food underground, the shrew-moles forage for the most part in the litter layer. They do construct burrows but these are shallow affairs made by compressing the loose soil into the tunnel walls. Without the need to

Figure 1.7 Scanning electron micrograph of the sensory vibrissae on the tail of a European mole (Photo: Martyn L. Gorman)

push heaps of spoil to the surface they do not produce the molehills so characteristic of the workings of 'true' moles. At an anatomical level the shrew-moles are not nearly so specialised for digging as are the New and Old World moles. In these latter animals the forelimbs have evolved into powerful digging tools and are turned permanently outwards from the body, like a pair of oars protruding from a rowing boat (Figure 1.2). The humerus is shortened and flattened, nearly as wide as it is long, and articulates with both the scapula and the clavicle. The large hands are almost circular in outline and are equipped with large, strong nails. The cylindrical body is covered in a dense fur of uniform length that lies with equal ease in any direction, a feature which must be a great comfort to a mole on those occasions when it needs to move backwards along its tunnel system! As in other mammals, the individual hairs leave the skin sloping diagonally backwards, but twisting and curling at the base allows them to move equally easily in any direction. In most species of moles, including the European mole *Talpa europaea*, the tail is relatively short, covered in hairs, which are sensory (Figure 1.7), and is held semi-erect. Held in this position, and brushing against the tunnel walls and roof, the tail is able to pick up a variety of information including vibrations passing through the soil. The tail is not just an early-warning system, however, and in some species it may be put to other uses. The star-nosed mole (*Condylura cristata*) of North America, for example, has a tail that is almost as long as its body and which seems to act as a store for fat to be utilised during the breeding season when energy demands can be unusually high.

10

Figure 1.8 *The distribution of the living species of talpid moles and desmans*

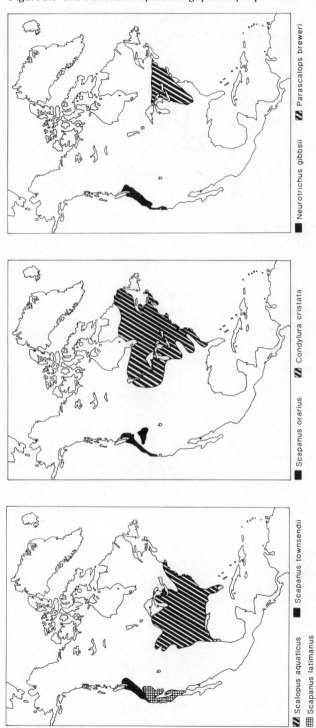

Figure 1.8 continued

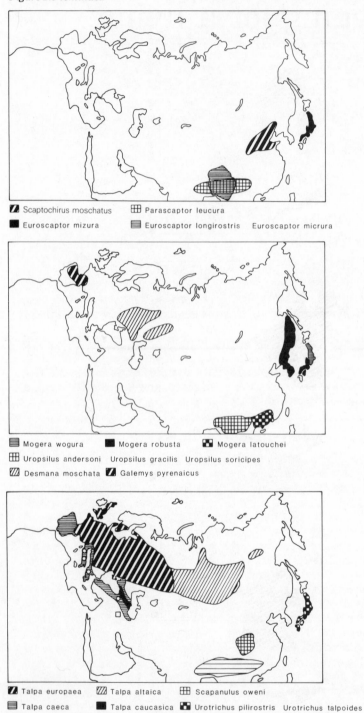

Scaptochirus moschatus   Parascaptor leucura

Euroscaptor mizura   Euroscaptor longirostris   Euroscaptor micrura

Mogera wogura   Mogera robusta   Mogera latouchei

Uropsilus andersoni   Uropsilus gracilis   Uropsilus soricipes

Desmana moschata   Galemys pyrenaicus

Talpa europaea   Talpa altaica   Scapanulus oweni

Talpa caeca   Talpa caucasica   Urotrichus pilirostris   Urotrichus talpoides

Scaptonyx fusicaudus   Talpa streeti   Talpa romana

2 Digging for a living

TYPES OF EARTHWORKS
AND HOW MOLES DIG THEM

As will become clear a little later, digging for a living can be pretty hard work at times. The kinds of earthworks that moles produce depend very much on the nature of the surroundings in which they find themselves; however the way in which they dig them depends upon their evolutionary history. One mole, digging near to Hampton Court in 1702, even managed to alter the course of British history. King William III was thrown to the ground when his horse, Sorrel, stumbled on the molehill. The king, already weak and ill, broke his collar-bone and died of pneumonia a few days later. Jacobites everywhere were delighted, and henceforth drank a toast to 'the little gentleman in the black velvet waistcoat'.

Chrysochlorid Moles

Probably the most formidable conditions for digging are those faced by the Namib golden mole *Eremitalpa granti namibensis*, searching for sand-dwelling lizards and invertebrates through the hot, shifting sands of the Namib Desert (Plate 2). This unfortunate mole faces a particularly uphill battle, for as soon as it excavates a space in the substratum, loose sand pours in and negates its efforts. Consequently, permanent tunnels and associated molehills are a rarity, restricted to areas of unusually wet or compacted ground (Roberts, 1951). Elsewhere all that can be seen at the surface are runs of disturbed and uplifted sand permeating across the dunes and marking where a mole has passed a few centimetres below. These surface runs are not permanent passages and new ones are continually being made until in some places the ground is covered with a network of raised dikes. Like all golden moles, the Namib mole digs both with its limbs and with its head, the muzzle being capped with a hard leathery pad (Figure 1.5). The forelimbs, each of which terminates in two greatly enlarged claws, are anatomically similar to those of normal running animals in that they hang down below the body and move forwards and backwards in the vertical plane (Figure 2.1). Golden moles, therefore, dig like the majority of other burrowing mammals, by

15

Figure 2.1 Skeleton of the forelimb of a golden mole

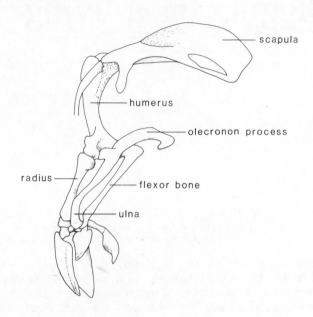

scratching at the ground with rapid running movements of the forelimbs, in the manner of a terrier dog.

In fact, thanks to the recent work of French scientists, we now know in great detail just how Namib moles dig, even when they are completely underground and hidden from normal view. Gasc *et al.* (1986) have used a form of X-ray photography, known as cinefluorography, to study the digging behaviour of this species. Sand is opaque to X-rays, but happily semolina is not and golden moles accept the fine-grained variety as a good substitute for the real thing! When placed on the surface of the sand, or semolina, a mole will plunge its head under the surface, and while bracing itself with its feet, will quickly dig itself in by means of rapid and successive movements of the forelimbs. Once safely under the surface, movement becomes much more difficult and demands a quite different digging strategy. Analysis of the X-ray films reveals that progression through the sand involves a repeated cycle of buttressing and propulsive movements (Figure 2.2). During the buttressing phase both forelimbs are fully extended forwards and the powerful claws locked into the ground. Thus anchored in the sea of sand, the mole pushes up its head and the anterior part of its body with great force, loosening and disturbing the sand in front of its snout whilst compacting it above and below its body. Both forelimbs are then thrust forwards together, under the chin and into the loosened sand before being pulled powerfully backwards together with the rear limbs. The result is not to throw sand behind the mole but rather to propel the animal bodily forwards, into the pocket of loosened sand. All four limbs are then brought forwards in readiness for the next power stroke. After 2–5 of these propulsive thrusts the sand is again loosened by a further upward thrust of the head and body.

Figure 2.2 Schematic drawing of the digging of the Namib golden mole (after Gasc et al., 1986)

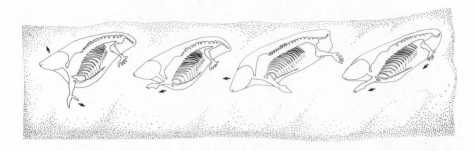

Happily for them not all golden moles live under such difficult conditions; other species inhabit a wide variety of habitats including grassveld, swampy areas, forests and mountains. In such places species like the Hottentot mole *Amblysomus hottentotus* not only make surface runs but are also able to dig permanent burrow systems consisting of many metres of tunnels lying 10–50 cm below the surface (Kuyper, 1985). The soil, which is often extremely hard, is loosened by the hands whilst the body is held firmly braced against the tunnel walls by the splayed feet (Puttick & Jarvis, 1977). The excavated soil is kicked back behind the animal by the legs until a suitable quantity has accumulated in the tunnel. The mole then turns or somersaults within the narrow confines of the burrow and with powerful thrusts of its forequarters commences to push the soil along the tunnel with its leathery snout. The soil tailings are either packed into old redundant tunnels or pushed up side shafts to the surface to form molehills. At one or more places within the burrow system, *Amblysomus* and other golden moles excavate a small spherical nesting chamber which is packed with leaves and grass. Here they sleep and, if female, raise their young.

Talpid Moles

The talpid moles generally inhabit well-structured soils in which it is possible to dig complex networks of permanent or semi-permanent tunnels. These moles do not dig with their heads in the way that golden moles do, but only with the forelimbs which are held out to the sides of the body with the broad, spadelike hands positioned vertically and facing backwards. The way in which talpid moles dig has been described in some detail for both the European mole *Talpa europaea* (Skoczen, 1958) and for the eastern American mole *Scalopus aquaticus* (Hisaw, 1923). The method of digging is quite unlike that of golden moles in that the front limbs move fore and aft in the *horizontal* plane in a manner akin to that of a human swimming using the breast-stroke. However, the analogy is only superficial for, as we shall see later, the underlying anatomies are very different indeed.

Talpid moles dig two main types of burrows, surface tunnels and deep tunnels (Figure 2.3). Surface tunnels are evident as raised dikes or disturbed soil running along the ground and are particularly common in

Figure 2.3 Generalised plan of the tunnel system of a talpid mole. Note that the vertical and horizontal scales are different (partly after Arlton, 1936)

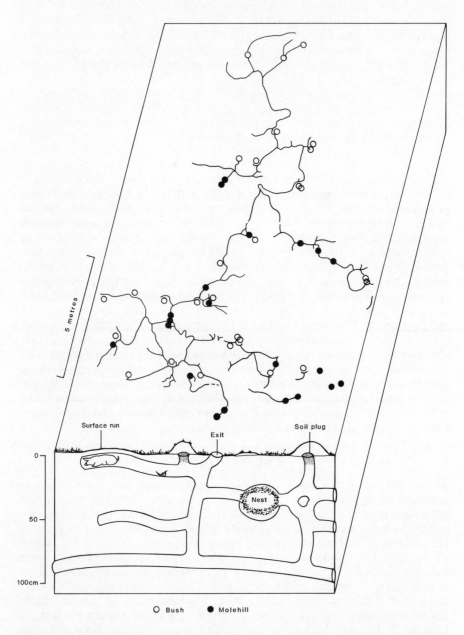

newly cultivated fields, in areas of light sandy soil and in very shallow soils where prey are concentrated just beneath the surface (Plate 10). Such tunnels are formed by moles digging a few centimetres beneath the surface of the ground. With no great weight of soil pressing down upon it from above the mole is able to push and compress the soil backwards and upwards with its forelimbs. Under these conditions there is no necessity for the formation of the spoil heaps we know as molehills (Plate 9). In particularly soft soils a mole may 'swim' through the soil in true breast-stroke fashion, using both forelimbs in synchrony. More usually, it digs with only one forelimb at a time with the body held firmly braced against the tunnel walls by the splayed hind limbs and the inactive forelimb. Soil is then sheared from the working face of the tunnel and pushed backwards and upwards by the active forelimb. After two or three strokes the roles of the two forelimbs are reversed. As the mole moves forward through the torn and loosened earth its body shapes the excavation into a smooth ovoid tunnel some 4–5 cm in cross-section.

Surface tunnels are, however, comparatively uncommon and short-lived structures; moles more usually dig tunnels further down in the soil column, particularly when the soil is deep or so dry that soil invertebrates have migrated down from the surface layers. In established territories the system of deep burrows consists of a complex branching network of hundreds of metres of tiered tunnels lying at various depths in the soil (Figure 2.3). The deeper tunnels are most used during times of drought or low temperatures when the soil invertebrates on which the mole feeds migrate deep into the soil. When digging these tunnels, which may lie anywhere from 5 to 150 cm below the surface, the mole cannot compress the excavated soil into the sides of the tunnel but must remove it to the surface (Figure 2.4). At these depths the mole shears the soil with alternate forepaws, its body being held securely against the walls of the tunnel with the hind limbs and the inactive forelimb. The excavated soil is thrown back behind it and down the tunnel by the digging forepaw, assisted by rapid scrabbling movements of the corresponding hind paw. Once a suitable volume of spoil has been accumulated the mole turns within the tight confines of the tunnel, either sideways or by somersaulting, and begins to push it back down the tunnel away from the working face. To do so, it places one of its forepaws diagonally to the body, rather like the offset blade of a bulldozer, and with two or three powerful thrusts of the body it moves the soil along the tunnel. It then changes over forepaws and continues its Herculean task until it reaches a previously dug side tunnel leading to the surface. The soil is pushed up this sloping lateral shaft and out onto the surface to form a molehill. The mole then returns to the tunnel face and continues to dig. At some point, of course, it becomes cheaper in terms of energy to dig a new lateral shaft to the surface rather than to continue to push soil down the ever lengthening tunnel. The spoil from the new lateral is pushed down into the main tunnel and is then transported to the old lateral tunnel, where it is either forced to the surface or used to pack the now redundant shaft.

The result of all this unseen labour is a line of molehills marking the route of the subterranean passage. The question of how a mole might decide when the time has come to dig a new lateral will be dealt with in a later section. Nevertheless, it should be noted that under some circumstances it may not be possible to dig shafts to the surface, and that then the mole must transport soil down quite long stretches of tunnel. A case in point concerns one of our study moles, a male with a large territory encompassing areas on both sides of the main A96 road from Peterhead to Aberdeen in north-east Scotland. When we attached a radio transmitter

Figure 2.4 A composite drawing of how the European mole digs: by first shearing soil from the tunnel face and then pushing it up a lateral shaft to the surface

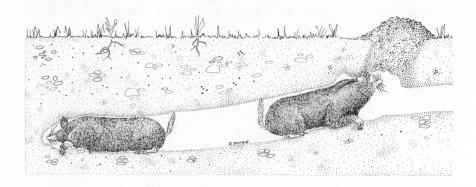

to this animal we were astonished to find that the two parts of its territory were connected by a single tunnel running under the entire width of the two-lane paved highway.

It must be emphasised that moles do not dig new tunnels each time they go out to forage for their daily food. Once dug, the deep permanent tunnels are repeatedly used for feeding over long periods of time, sometimes indeed by several generations of moles. In undisturbed populations the number of molehills in an area gives little or no indication of the number of moles present and therefore cannot be used as an index of mole density. Indeed, permanent pastures supporting very high densities of moles may bear no molehills for much of the year. Once a territory has become established, molehills appear only when and where the tunnel system is being extended or repaired following damage by frost or flooding, and they give no clue as to the true extent of the individual's home range.

Within their tunnel systems moles construct one or more spherical nest chambers. They pack each with a ball of shredded dry material (Plate 13) which is collected either by pulling plants by their roots into the tunnels, or by taking them from the surface in the vicinity of a tunnel exit. Most nests contain dry grass and leaves but moles will use whatever material is available. For example, many contain newspaper or pieces of plastic sheeting while one nest that we excavated in a field behind a village pub consisted entirely of discarded crisp packets! The nest is used for sleeping and in the case of females for raising the young to weaning.

The vast majority of molehills are relatively small and without internal structure. On occasion, though, European moles construct large and structured mounds containing upwards of 750 kg of soil (Skoczen, 1961). These edifices, which represent an enormous investment of energy by the mole, are known rather romantically as 'fortresses' (Plates 11 and 12). They are built by both males and females and may be used at any time of the year, but particularly from late autumn to spring. Some females give birth inside their fortresses. Although fortresses can be found almost anywhere, they are particularly common where very shallow soils overlie hard impenetrable subsoils and in areas prone to

Figure 2.5 A cross-section through the fortress of a European mole showing the nest chamber (N) and a network of eleven tunnels

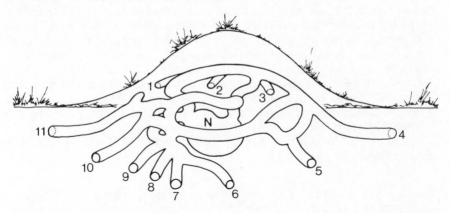

flooding. Internally, fortresses almost always contain one or more nest chambers, which are situated at or above ground level, a network of tunnels of varying complexity, and in some cases a sump leading to drinking water (Figure 2.5). They may also contain stores of food. During the autumn and winter moles often collect earthworms and after immobilising them by biting off their head segments, they hoard them in caches (Evans, 1948; Skoczen, 1961). The harvested worms may be placed in custom-built chambers dug near to the nest, they may be inserted individually or in small groups into the walls of the tunnels, or they may be stored within the fortress itself (Figure 2.6). There they remain until either they are eaten by the mole or the soil temperature rises in the

Figure 2.6 European moles make caches of beheaded worms in the walls of tunnels in the fortress (1), in the nest chamber (2), in the walls of the permanent tunnels (3) and in chambers built especially for this purpose (4) (after Skoczen, 1961)

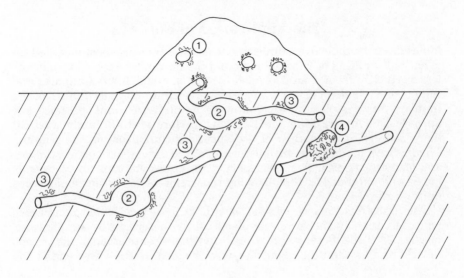

spring when they disperse, their head segments having by then regenerated. Moles appear to be very selective in their choice of worms for storage since the species composition of caches is quite different from that of the worm community at large. For example, in areas of Poland a single species, *Lumbricus terrestris*, accounted for 90 per cent of stored worms but less than 25 per cent of the free-living earthworm community in the surrounding area (Skoczen, 1961). The quantity of worms stored within a fortress can be surprisingly large and represents a most valuable food store; the Polish caches excavated by Skoczen (1961) contained up to 1.6 kg of worms while Stone and Vogel (unpublished data) report figures of over 2 kg from fortresses in Switzerland, again mainly *L. terrestris*. We shall return to the vexing question of the function of the fortress later in this chapter.

THE ANATOMY OF DIGGING

All fossorial mammals tend to be compact, stocky creatures whose heads merge into their cylindrical bodies with little external evidence of a neck. Their limbs are short and, in the case of the forelimbs, largely confined within the general contours of the body. Usually, they are covered in a short dense fur which stands upright and which can be brushed in any direction with equal ease. Overall, they lack all those external features which might in any way hinder their easy passage through the soil. These modifications are only the tip of the iceberg, however, because the muscular and skeletal adaptations that lie below are, if anything, yet more striking. Their *raison d'être* is to provide a digging tool for shearing and shifting soil and the means to exert and apply the very large forces that these activities demand. The strength of these little mammals is quite prodigious. *Scalopus aquaticus*, for example, can exert a force equivalent to 32 times its own body weight (Arlton, 1936) while a 57 g golden mole is on record as having escaped from captivity by moving aside a 9.5 kg iron cover (Bateman, 1959)!

The Application of Force

Moles dig with their front limbs and it is these that are most modified. In a 'normal' walking or running mammal the forelimb hangs down more or less vertically from a joint formed by the shoulder blade (scapula) and collar-bone (clavicle) (Figure 2.7). The movement and musculature of the limb are very complex, but the following simplified account will serve our purpose. During walking the limb swings fore and aft in the vertical plane largely by movement of the upper leg (humerus) on the scapula. The muscles mainly responsible for the power stroke are the *teres major* and *latissimus dorsi*. The lower part of the limb, the ulna and radius, is flexed and extended at the elbow by the action of the biceps and triceps muscles respectively.

The limb thus consists of a series of bony levers activated by muscles and consequently the forces involved can be described by simple lever mechanics. Take, for example, the elbow where contraction of the triceps muscle rotates the ulna about the pivot formed by the lower end of the

Figure 2.7 The forelimb skeleton and musculature of the dog, a typical running mammal. See text for further details

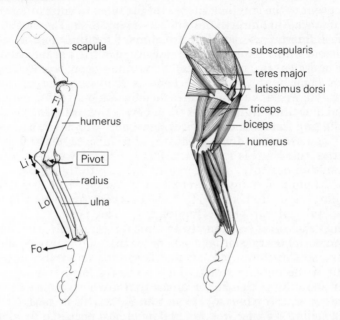

humerus (Figure 2.7). The in-force exerted by the muscle (F_i) is related to the out-force applied by the end of the limb (F_o) as follows

$$F_i \times L_i = F_o \times L_o$$
or
$$F_o = \frac{F_i \times L_i}{L_o}$$

where L_i is the distance from the muscle insertion to the pivot and L_o is the distance from the pivot to the other end of the bone.

The term that interests us most is F_o, the force applied to the ground by the limb. A fossorial mammal can increase the magnitude of this force by increasing F_i, by increasing L_i or by decreasing L_o. In fact moles have gone down all three avenues: they have large muscles when compared to non-digging relatives; these muscles insert relatively far from the joints they turn; and the length of their digging tool, the hand and forearm, is relatively short.

Golden moles are scratch diggers. They dig by extending their forearms, which are tipped with three strong blade-like claws, into the earth before dragging them downwards and under the body with considerable force. Each forelimb has four digits; the claws on the third digits are strongly formed, those on the first and second less so, and the fourth digits in most species are mere stumps (Figure 2.1). The claws are sharply pointed and hollow underneath so that their edges act like a wood-carver's chisel for cutting through the soil. In golden moles the forelimbs move backwards and forwards like those of walking mammals, but they are specialised to provide great strength in extending the elbow and when flexing the digits and wrist, the main digging actions. The lever arm to which the triceps is attached, the olecranon process of the ulna, is very long indeed. In most golden moles it is equivalent to about 75 per cent of the length of the rest of the ulna, as compared to only 15 per cent in a walking insectivore, such as a hedgehog. The medial epicondyle of the humerus, the point of attachment for the muscles that flex the digits and wrist, is massive and indicative of their great strength. One of these muscles, the deep digital flexor, has been largely replaced by a robust bone. One end of the bone is firmly anchored to the medial epicondyle while the other is attached by tendons to the undersides of the second and third digits. When the elbow is flexed during the later stages of a digging stroke, the bone is dragged backwards and downwards away from the forearm and wrist, causing the claws to flex and to bite deeply into the soil. By this means the force of the powerful biceps muscle is transmitted not only to the forearm but also to the digits.

The talpid moles dig in a very different way. Their forelimbs stick out at right angles from the body and are swept from front to back in the horizontal, lateral plane (Figure 2.4). The power to force the hand through the soil is transmitted in a most remarkable way, by rotation of the humerus. Extension and flexion of the elbow provide no propulsive power and serve only to raise and lower the hand, thus controlling the height of the digging action. Such a bizarre form of movement implies major anatomical changes, changes that are seen at their most extreme in the genera *Scapanus*, *Scalopus* and *Talpa* (Reed, 1951; Yalden, 1966). The scapulae are long and thin and lie almost horizontally along the back of the mole (Figures 2.8 and 2.9). The breastbone is long and the clavicles

Figure 2.8 The forelimb skeleton and musculature of the European mole

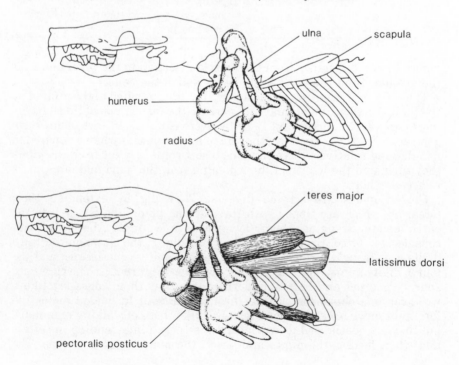

Figure 2.9 Lateral view of the skeleton of a European mole (Photo: Andrew Lucas)

clavicles short and robust with the result that the shoulder joints lie very far forward, close together and low down under the neck.

The humerus of a mole is quite typical; it is a massively built bone, short but very broad and equipped with strong muscle insertions (Figure 2.10). It is one of those anatomical specimens that once seen is never forgotten. Its orientation in the living animal is as unusual as is its morphology. Instead of hanging downwards from its point of articulation at the shoulder it points upwards and outwards! The broad humerus is rather like a sagging door, hinged only at the bottom and leaning out at the top, away from the door jamb. The elbow joint is oriented so that the forearm sticks out sideways from the upper (anatomically lower!) end of the humerus with the hand held vertically, its palm facing outwards and backwards ready to sweep against the tunnel wall. The hand itself is large, broad and thick and the digits are more or less webbed with tough skin. The width of the hand of the more specialised moles, such as *Talpa*, is further increased by the presence of the falciform bone which acts as a sixth digit.

The major muscles responsible for the digging stroke, the *teres major*, *pectoralis*, *posticus*, *subscapularis* and *latissimus dorsi*, are all large and attached to the outer edge of the humerus or, to continue our analogy with a door, the edge with the handle (Figure 2.8). The other ends of the muscles insert on the breastbone and shoulder-blade. When they contract they cause the humerus to rotate about its long vertical axis, exactly in like opening a door. The result is to pull the forearm backwards in a horizontal sweeping motion. Because the humerus is so broad and because the muscles insert at the opposite side to where it pivots on its

25

Figure 2.10 The evolution of the mole humerus, showing two lineages in which the humerus greatly increases in width, thus increasing the power of the rotational digging stroke. The upper lineage represents extinct forms (after Savage & Long, 1986)

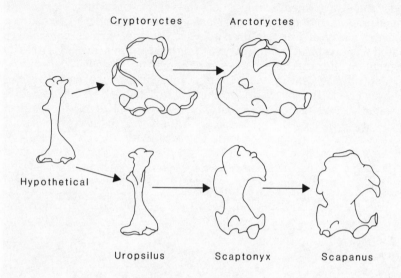

joint, the lever arm (L_i) is effectively very long. Coupled with the short forearm and powerful muscles, this provides a very large out-force at the hand.

THE COSTS OF DIGGING

We have just described how moles are morphologically adapted to exert the very large forces that are required to shear and to shift soil successfully. In this section it will be shown that the exertion of these forces requires the expenditure of a considerable amount of energy. First of all, we shall set the scene by discussing how energy expenditure is measured in animals and by defining the units that are used. We shall then look at the costs of normal locomotion as a benchmark against which to view the costs of digging.

Animals obey the first law of thermodynamics in that they can neither create nor destroy energy. It follows from this that what goes into an animal must eventually come out. This can be expressed rather more formally by the balanced growth equation:

$$
\begin{aligned}
\text{ingestion} = \ &\text{growth} \\
&+ \text{reproduction} \\
&+ \text{excretion} \\
&+ \text{egestion} \\
&+ \text{respiration}
\end{aligned}
$$

The term that is of most concern at this point is respiration, the oxidation of organic molecules to carbon dioxide and water with the release of energy to power the machinery of the animal. The rate of respiration of an animal, its metabolic rate (R), is a measure of the amount of work being performed at any given time.

Respiration can be quantified, often with great accuracy, by a variety of methods including measurement of the rates at which oxygen is consumed and carbon dioxide is released. In the biological literature a bewildering array of units is used to measure the various parameters associated with respiration: milligrams (mg), millilitres (ml) and litres (l) for oxygen; milligrams, grams (g) and kilograms (kg) for body mass; seconds (s), minutes (min), hours (h) and days (d) for time; calories, (cal) kilocalories (kcal) and joules (J) for energy. In this book we have tried to be consistent in our use of units and have expressed size in kilograms of living material, energy in joules and the rate at which energy is used in watts, i.e. an energy flux of one joule per second (Js^{-1}).

A minimal metabolic rate, measured in a conscious animal which is inactive, unexcited, healthy, fasting, non-reproducing and not expending energy to keep itself warm nor to cool itself, is known as the basal metabolic rate (R_b or BMR). This represents the minimum power required to keep the basic machinery of life ticking over. An additional activity by the animal, even standing, will of course increase its energy demands. The maximum metabolic rate at which a particular species can operate, measured in individuals trained to exercise on treadmills, is usually less than ten times the basal rate. These upper rates are rarely achieved by free-living animals who spend most of their lives at an intermediate value between basal and maximum rates, known as the average realised rate of metabolism. This is usually two to three times the basal rate.

The metabolic rate of an animal also depends upon its body-weight or mass. The larger it is, the greater the rate at which it expends energy. Unfortunately the two are not related in a simple linear fashion (Peters, 1983). Instead, like other body-weight relationships, they conform to the following general equation:

$$Y = aW^b \quad \text{(Equation 1)}$$

where Y is the biological phenomenon in question, in this case the metabolic rate, W is body-weight and a and b are constants that can be obained by measurement or experimentation. When Y is plotted against W, this equation does not describe a straight line, except when b takes the value 1, and this is rarely the case.

Hemmingsen (1960) has shown that, across a wide range of warm-blooded animals, the relationship between basal metabolic rate (in watts) and body-weight (in kilograms) is described by

$$R_b = 4.1W^{0.75} \quad \text{(Equation 2)}$$

Movement, of course, requires the expenditure of energy and leads to an increase in the metabolic rate of an animal, usually by a large factor. The costs of locomotion have been measured for a wide variety of species, usually by measuring their oxygen demands whilst they are exercising on some form of treadmill at known velocities. These results can, once again, be described by a single curve (Peters, 1983) that gives the moving metabolic rate of a walking or running animal at any given velocity:

$$R_m = 1.2R_b + V11.3W^{0.72} \quad \text{(Equation 3)}$$

where R_m is the metabolic rate whilst running (in watts), R_b is the basal metabolic rate (in watts) and is multiplied by 1.2 to correct for the postural costs of standing erect, V the velocity (ms^{-1}), and W is the body-weight (in kilograms).

Substituting the value for R_b from Equation 2 gives

$$R_m = 4.92W^{0.75} + V11.3W^{0.72} \quad \text{(Equation 4)}$$

Division of the moving metabolic rate (R_m) by the velocity gives the cost of transport (T_c), the energy expended by the animal in moving over a particular distance and measured, in our case, in joules per metre (Jm^{-1}).

$$T_c = \frac{R_m}{V}$$

$$= \frac{(4.92W^{0.75})}{V} + 11.3W^{0.72} \quad \text{(Equation 5)}$$

A close examination of Equations 4 and 5 reveals that although moving metabolic rates rise with increasing velocity, nevertheless transport costs, the energy expended per unit of distance, decline at higher speeds. Indeed, in terms of energy expenditure the most efficient speed is the maximum that the animal can achieve and maintain.

Having covered this groundwork we can now return to the major question that we wish to address: how much energy is expended by moles when digging their tunnels? David Vleck of the University of Arizona has successfully solved the technically difficult problem of measuring the respiratory rates of actively burrowing mammals. To do so, he introduces the animals into plastic cylinders packed with soil, through which air is made to flow at an accurately known rate (Figure 2.11). The metabolic rate of the animal can then be calculated from measurements of the difference between the oxygen content of the air entering and leaving the

Figure 2.11 Measuring the costs of digging by means of respirometry (after Vleck, 1979)

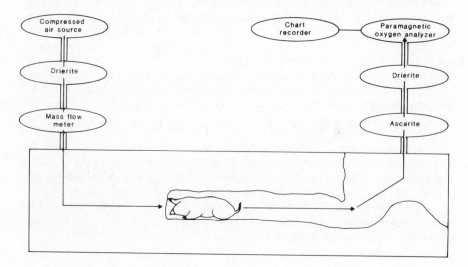

respirometer. Vleck (1979) first used the system to measure the cost of burrowing in a fossorial rodent, the pocket gopher *Thomomys bottae*. This species digs by scratching in essentially the same way as the golden moles we described earlier. Subsequent measurements have also been made of the cost of digging in the North American mole *Scapanus townsendii* (Vleck and Kenagy, manuscript). This species quickly started to dig tunnels when placed in the respirometer, shearing soil loose and then turning around to push the spoil back down the cylinder.

The metabolic rates of digging gophers were on average 4.1 times those of resting animals, a considerable increase. The construction of one metre of tunnel of radius 3.5 cm required an expenditure of 3,300 J in sandy soil and a massive 30,000 J in a cohesive clay (Vleck, 1979). These figures can be put into perspective by comparing them to the energy that is expended by a gopher moving on the surface or through existing tunnels. From Equation 5 it would be predicted that a 150 g animal, moving at a velocity of 0.25 ms^{-1}, would incur a transport cost of only 7.62 Jm^{-1}. Thus even in the most friable of soils the cost of burrowing far exceeds the cost of normal locomotion; to dig one metre of tunnel requires between 400 and 4,000 times as much energy as does walking for the same distance on the surface. The cost of digging was similarly high for the mole where the digging of one metre of tunnel through an alluvial soil involved an expenditure of over 5,000 J. The comparable cost of walking through existing tunnels would have been 9.1 Jm^{-1} for an individual of *S. townsendii* with a body-weight of 120 g.

In these beautifully elegant experiments it also proved possible to divide the total cost of digging into two components, the cost associated with shearing soil from the working face and that involved in pushing the soil along the tunnel to the surface. In the case of the mole, the shearing of one kg of soil cost in the region of 450 J whilst pushing the same amount for a distance of one metre involved an expenditure of some 1,500–2,500 J.

Since the energy costs of digging tunnels are so very high one might expect that moles would dig them in a way that minimises those costs. Vleck (1981) has developed a model of digging which allows us to investigate whether in fact fossorial animals do dig in the most economical manner. Although originally developed to simulate the digging behaviour of pocket gophers the model is equally applicable to moles.

We described earlier the way in which moles dig their deep tunnels in sections, each segment comprising a length of tunnel proper and an associated lateral shaft up which the excavated soil is removed to the surface. The model allows us to address the central problem facing the mole, namely when does it become more economic to dig a new lateral rather than to continue pushing soil down the ever lengthening tunnel to the preceding one? The simulation assumes that a mole begins a new segment by digging a sloping lateral shaft to the surface and that it uses the soil thus excavated to plug the preceding lateral (Figure 2.12). A length of tunnel is then dug out and the spoil is pushed up the new lateral to the surface to form a molehill. The cost of digging the tunnel includes, therefore, the cost of digging the lateral shafts and of raising the soil against gravity.

Figure 2.12 Diagrammatic representation of the tunnel of a European mole. D is the depth of the main tunnel, L the length of the lateral shaft, and S the segment length between one lateral shaft and the next (after Vleck, 1981)

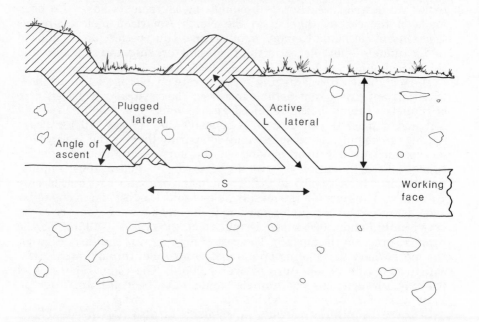

The mass of soil removed per metre of tunnel (M) is given by $\pi r^2 d$ where r is the radius of the tunnel and d the bulk density of the soil. The total mass of soil removed from a segment of tunnel including its associated lateral is thus $M \times (S+L)$ where S and L are the segment and lateral lengths in metres.

The soil from the tunnel itself, a mass of $M \times S$ is pushed a mean distance of $0.5S+L$ to the surface and is raised a distance of D against gravity. The soil from the lateral, a mass of $M \times L$ is pushed a distance of $S+L$ and is raised a mean distance of $0.5D$ against gravity.

If the cost of shearing soil is K_s (J kg^{-1}) and the cost of pushing soil is K_p (J kg^{-1} m^{-1}) then the total cost of excavating a segment of tunnel is:

$$M(S+L)K_s + M(S) (0.5S+ L)K_p + M(L) (S+L)K_p + 5 (M.S.g.D) + 5(M.L.g.0.5D)$$

where g is the acceleration due to gravity. (The cost of raising soil against gravity has been multiplied by 5 to take into account the fact that energy expended by animals in doing work against gravity is only 20 per cent efficient).

The model can be used to investigate the effect of segment length on the costs of digging tunnels at different depths (Figure 2.13). The curves in this figure are based on parameters from real tunnel systems of European moles excavated in north-east Scotland. One tunnel system lay an average of 15.1 cm below the ground, the other 45.3 cm. The tunnels had an average diameter of 5.5 cm and the lateral shafts ascended to the surface at a mean angle of 45 degrees to the horizontal. Both systems had been dug in the same field through a clay soil having a density of

Figure 2.13 The economics of digging by European moles. The histograms show the frequency distribution of distances between adjacent molehills, and thus lateral shafts, for tunnels at two different depths. The smooth curves represent the predicted costs of digging tunnels, at these two depths, as a function of the distance between lateral shafts

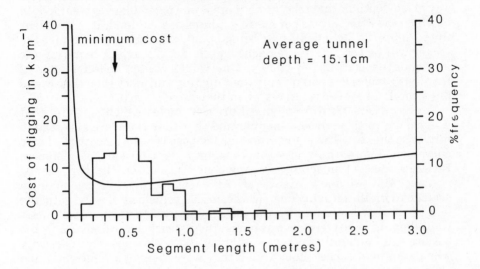

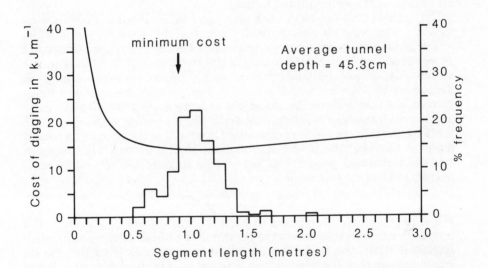

1.5 g cc^{-1}. We have assumed that the costs of shearing and pushing soil would be similar to those measured by Vleck and Kenagy for the similarly sized *S. townsendii*.

The results show that if a mole were to dig its tunnel in very short segments then the cost of construction, in terms of energy expended per metre of tunnel, would be very high since of course the animal would have to dig a lot of laterals. If it digs it in longer segments, with fewer laterals, the amount of soil to be sheared and removed decreases and so the cost begins to drop. However, as the distance between laterals increases, the soil must be pushed along the tunnel for greater and greater distances and thus the cost begins to rise again. Consequently, for any given depth in the soil column there is one particular segment length at which the energy costs per metre of tunnel are minimal. It is also clear from Figure 2.13 that, all else being equal, the deeper the tunnel the longer will be the optimal segment length, i.e. the length requiring the minimum expenditure of energy. One would predict therefore that if free-living moles are maximising their digging efficiency then they would dig laterals at longer intervals when they dig deeper tunnels.

We have data from free-living European moles which suggests that they do dig in this efficient manner and that they therefore also tend to minimise the cost. The histograms superimposed on the smooth predicted curves in Figure 2.13 are the frequency distributions of distances between adjacent molehills (i.e. segment lengths) on the two burrow systems that we have excavated. At each depth the most common segment length actually dug by the moles coincided closely with the length predicted to minimise the cost in energy. Moreover, when moles were digging relatively deep tunnels, they struck lateral shafts to the surface less frequently than when digging shallower ones. This is exactly what one would expect them to do if they were digging as efficiently and cheaply as possible. Clearly moles do not dig blindly, but have an acute awareness of the economics of mining!

Not only do moles have to work very hard when digging, they must do so while breathing air that is low in oxygen and high in carbon dioxide. Above ground at sea level the oxygen content of the atmosphere is around 21 per cent, but in the fetid tunnel of the coast mole it is usually in the region of 16–20 per cent and can drop to as little as 6 per cent (Schaefer & Sadleir, 1979). The concentrations of carbon dioxide are up to ten times those of the atmosphere. As one might expect, moles are well adapted to dealing with this problem, right down to the molecular level.

Moles contain twice as much blood and twice as much of the red pigment haemoglobin as other mammals of similar size. Haemoglobin has the important property of being able to combine reversibly with oxygen to form oxyhaemoglobin.

$$Hb + 4O_2 \rightleftharpoons Hb4O_2$$

When haemoglobin is exposed to high concentrations of oxygen in the lungs the reaction is forced to the right and the blood becomes saturated. However, when the blood leaves the lungs and travels to the tissues where oxygen tensions are low, the reaction goes to the left and oxygen is released. Figure 2.14 shows a graph of how the percentage saturation of rat haemoglobin changes as it is exposed to different partial pressures of oxygen. The result, known as a dissociation curve, is typically sigmoid in shape. Dissociation curves differ from one species to the next but most, like that of the rat, would be contained within the shaded area in Figure 2.14. However, a few species have curves which fall well to the left of the normal range. The blood of species such as these has a particularly high affinity for oxygen, and their haemoglobin is able to take it up readily, even at low partial pressures (Figure 2.14). Animals with haemoglobin of

Figure 2.14 Oxygen dissociation curves of haemoglobin for a range of mammals. The curves of species living in environments low in oxygen, e.g. the mole and llama, lie to the left of those of other species. This means that they have a higher affinity for oxygen and take it up readily, even at low partial pressures

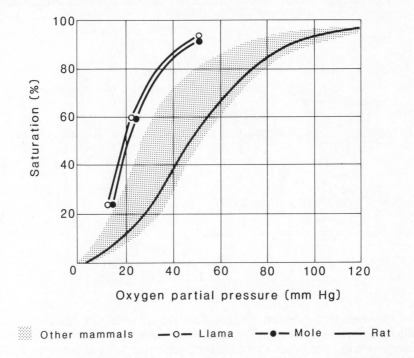

this kind are to be found in places lacking in oxygen, for example, the llama living at high altitudes in the Andes, and our friend the mole living below the ground (Jelkmann *et al.*, 1981).

THE RIDDLE OF THE FORTRESS

We shall conclude this chapter by returning to that most impressive and enigmatic of earthworks, the fortress of the European mole. Clearly, the old mole-catchers and countrymen who gave the structure this name looked upon it as a fortified retreat to be used in times of crisis. We are of the opinion that they were perfectly correct, and that the fortress does indeed act as a victualled refuge for a mole under seige, not by its conspecifics, but by the forces of cold and water.

Fortresses are found in the greatest numbers in areas with a high water table, which are liable to flooding. When the waters rise the mole can retreat from the waterlogged tunnels and take refuge within the fortress. There it can remain, dry in its nest and sustained by the stores of worms, until the waters recede.

Fortresses are also a feature of shallow soils lying on a hard substrate. When they can, moles place their nests far down in the soil column, where temperatures are relatively stable and for most of the year rather

Figure 2.15 Seasonal changes in the temperature at 9 a.m. at different depths in the soil (Data courtesy of the Meteorological Office)

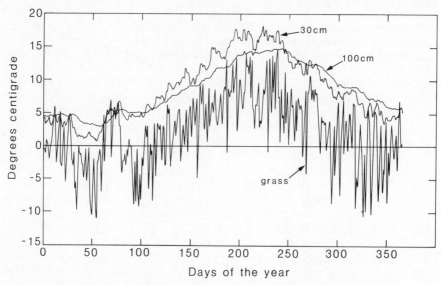

Temperatures on grass, at 30cm & at 100cm at Bush, Edinburgh

higher than at the surface (Figure 2.15). Moles living in thin soils cannot dig deep nests and are thus forced to sleep near the surface where temperatures are much more variable and nearer to those found above ground. Under these circumstances a fortress may offer a degree of insulation to the mole asleep in its nest. Furthermore, thin soils can freeze solid in winter, so that moles are unable to dig. With their prey immobilised in the icy soil, moles then face a bleak and hungry time. At such times the fortress offers a source of food and an insulated place to sleep.

We shall shortly examine these ideas in more detail, in particular the questions of how long stored worms will sustain a beseiged mole, and just how effective the insulation afforded by the fortress really is. Before doing so, we shall attempt to calculate the cost to the mole of building one of these megachthonic structures.

The Cost

It is very difficult to present a precise estimate of the cost of constructing a fortress, partly because they are so variable in their internal structure but mainly because there is insufficient information on how moles build them. However, it should be possible to come up with a reasonable estimate.

It can safely be assumed that a fortress is built with the soil excavated from tunnels that would have been dug anyway, as part of the general burrow system. What is of interest here is the extra cost the mole incurs in moving this large quantity of soil to one central point. The first task

34

therefore must be to calculate the length of tunnel needed to provide sufficient material for the construction of one of these great heaps. An average fortress has a volume of around 0.39m³ (Skoczen, 1961) and a mass, given soil with a bulk density of 1.5 g cc⁻¹, of some 586 kg. Since the spoil from one metre of tunnel weighs around 3.56 kg, building a fortress requires the material from 165 m of tunnel.

Normally, several tunnels radiate out from a fortress (Figure 2.5). For this analysis, let us consider the typical case of a fortress with five such tunnels and let us assume that the soil from which it is built has been excavated from the first 33 m of each of them. The cost of the fortress is the difference between the cost of digging the 165 m of tunnel in segments of the most economical length (see above) and the cost of digging them in five 33 m segments. It is possible, of course, to use the digging model described earlier to calculate these costs. For a tunnel system at a depth of 15 cm, the most economical strategy is to dig the tunnel in segments of 0.5 m at a total cost of 1,027 kJ. In contrast the more expensive method costs a staggering 15,180 kJ. Thus the extra work involved in the construction of a fortress requires an energy expenditure of some 14,153 kJ by the mole. The scale of the investment will be appreciated if we point out that this is equivalent to the total amount of energy expended by a 0.1 kg animal in carrying out its normal activities over a period of 72 days! That is a clearly a very large investment of energy, but, as they say in Yorkshire, 'Wot costs nowt's worth nowt'.

How Long Will the Stores Last?

European moles are very lean creatures and rarely have more than 3 g of fat stored in their bodies (Figure 2.16). These reserves will not last for very long if a mole is unable to feed because the ground is flooded or frozen. One gram of fat provides 39.7 kJ of energy and thus the typical fat

Figure 2.16 Seasonal changes in the average fat content of European moles from north-east Scotland

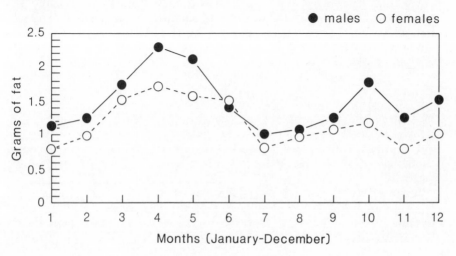

reserves of an adult will be depleted in less than 36 hours even if the animal is just ticking over at its basal metabolic rate. In fact, an animal holed up in its fortress will be using energy to keep warm and thus its fat deposits will be used up even more rapidly. Given such scant endogenous reserves, the caches of worms stored within the fortress are clearly central to the prolonged survival of the besieged mole. The most commonly stored species is *Lumbricus terrestris* which has an energy content of 2.947 kJ g^{-1} of live worm. The caches themselves can weigh as much as 1,500 g, an energy source of the order of 4,500 kJ. A reserve of this magnitude would sustain a 0.1 kg mole for 24 days if it were to continue to expend energy at the normal, average realised metabolic rate. However, a mole is likely to remain relatively inactive during such difficult times and thus the reserves will in practice last for substantially longer.

Is the Fortress a Good Insulator?

For any particular level of activity the rate of energy expenditure by an animal is least at an ambient temperature where loss of heat to the environment is minimal. At lower ambient temperatures increasing amounts of energy are used to maintain body temperature, even if the animal remains otherwise inactive. As an example, Figure 2.18 shows the metabolic response to decreasing temperatures of the hairy-tailed mole *Parascalops breweri* (Jensen, 1983).

Since moles normally spend more than half their lives asleep in their nests (see Chapter 5) it makes sense that they should be well insulated against heat loss, thus reducing energy expenditure. Does the fortress have a significant role to play in achieving this, in particular in the case of nests lying near to the surface on thin soils? In order to investigate this question we made use of an electronic analogue of a mole. This consisted of a thermostatically controlled heating element encased in epoxy resin and mounted in the freeze-dried carcass of a European mole (Figure 2.17).

Figure 2.17 The electronic mole used to investigate the thermal insulatory properties of mole nests and fortresses

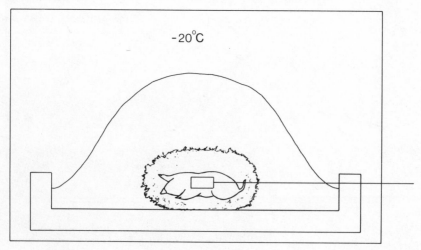

The 100 g 'mole' was maintained at a constant temperature of 37°C by means of a control box which also served to measure the power consumption of the model in watts. The experiments were designed to simulate the situation where a mole, faced with freezing conditions, had retreated into its fortress. It was assumed that once inside it would remain inactive in its nest, thus minimising its energy expenditure. Initially, the 'mole' was placed in the centre of a mass of nesting material and covered with 10 cm of soil before measuring its energy demands at a range of temperatures from +20°C to −20°C. The increase in the energy consumption of the 'mole' as it was subjected to decreasing ambient temperatures was linear and reflected closely the metabolic behaviour of a real mole (Figure 2.18). The 'mole', still swaddled in its nest material, was then covered with sufficient soil to form a relatively small fortress some 150 cm in diameter and 100 cm high. The measurements of energy consumption were then repeated over the same range of ambient temperatures, starting at the highest and allowing the fortress to equilibrate for 24 hours at each new temperature. The results were quite dramatic in that the covering of soil provided an appreciable degree of insulation and led to a decrease in energy consumption of over 30 per cent (Figure 2.17). The insulation given to a nest by a fortress is thus very real and is sufficiently marked to make an important contribution to the energy budget of the mole.

Figure 2.18 The relationship between energy expenditure and ambient temperature for a real mole Parascalops breweri and the electronic mole shown in Figure 2.17 (data for P. breweri from Jensen, 1983)

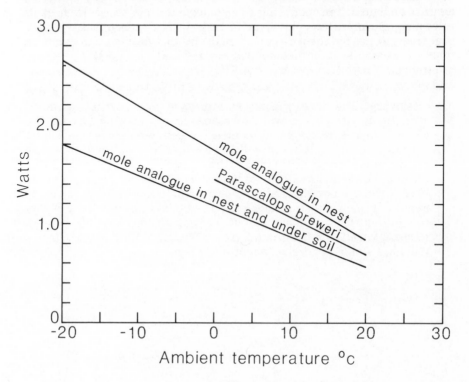

CAN MOLES DO ANYTHING ELSE BUT DIG?

Both talpid and chrysochlorid moles are so highly adapted for a fossorial existence that one might imagine that they are incapable of any form of locomotory activity other than digging. In fact, all moles can swim if they have to, albeit slowly and with little style. The fur of moles is relatively waterproof and tends to retain large amounts of air, thus rendering them rather buoyant. The result is that moles can swim for considerable periods and distances before tiring. Hickman (1988) has measured the endurance of a variety of species and has found that most can swim for 30–50 minutes, during which time they can cover distances of over a kilometre. This unexpected swimming ability goes some way towards explaining the mystery of how moles have colonised offshore islands, and must be of distinct survival value to moles living in areas prone to flooding. The moles living in the English fens are particularly vulnerable since the area can be covered by up to a metre of water several times per year (Mellanby, 1971). At such times the moles have to swim to high ground and wait for the floods to subside. One species, the star-nosed mole of North America, is actually semi-aquatic, spending part of its time underground and part underwater, obtaining food from both environments (Plates 3 and 4, Figure 1.6). Usually this mole digs its tunnels near to marshy ground and often they exit directly into open water. Both the front and rear limbs are used in swimming and the feet, although not webbed, are longer and wider than those of other species. The tail is unusually long and robust for a mole and may be used as a rudder.

Perhaps even more surprisingly, some moles appear to be accomplished cragsmen! Thus Hickman (1982) was somewhat nonplussed when upon releasing a trapped star-nosed mole he saw it climb vertically up a concrete wall to a height of 60 cm before eventually falling off. Even more impressed was the radio listener who in 1981 wrote to a BBC wildlife programme. The letter speaks for itself!

> My Burmese cat, who is a mighty hunter, brought in a mole a few weeks ago. The mole, which was a most valiant creature, climbed straight up the plaster wall to escape. It was making fast for the ceiling when I saw it and I went off to get some gloves (foolishly, perhaps, I couldn't bring myself to pick if off the wall with my bare hands) to prevent it hitting the ceiling and falling to the floor. I was too late, however, as when I got back it was lying on the carpet on its back. I removed and locked up the cat, who was looking at it rather nervously, picked up the mole and put it on its tum on a flower bed in the garden. Half an hour later it had gone, so presumably it must have dug itself into the ground. Are there any other records of moles climbing walls? It climbed about eight feet.

off and bolted down. However, despite such crude butchery, the meal is also eaten with a certain degree of finesse; an earthworm makes for a gritty feast at best and a mole will often clean one by squeezing it through its fingers as it eats, forcing most of the soil from the gut, like toothpaste from a tube (Arlton, 1936). Such behaviour presumably evolved as a mechanism to reduce excessive tooth wear, but in more recent times it has come to the aid of the mole in another, rather unexpected way. The earth-moving activities of moles can be a minor blight on the lives of farmers and gardeners, and inevitably provoke a degree of retaliation. The current methods of control are by trapping and, more usually, by poisoning with strychnine. The use of strychnine is problematical on a number of accounts. It is a cruel poison that causes great suffering, and poisoned moles dying on the surface of the ground may be eaten by carnivores and birds of prey which succumb in their turn. In addition, an unknown but probably significant quantity of strychnine is used illegally to kill a variety of other species which are regarded by some as vermin. These problems cause great concern in the United Kingdom and scientists of the Ministry of Agriculture, Food and Fisheries (MAFF) have put much effort into seeking more humane and selective poisons. Earthworms dusted in poison make the very best bait but unfortunately the food-cleaning behaviour of the mole tends to remove much of the chemical, making it difficult to administer a lethal dose. Faced with such formidable defensive measures the nonplussed scientists have been reduced to seeking methods of gluing the poisons to the outsides of the worms!

In some parts of the world earthworms are the most important component in the diet of moles throughout the entire year. For example, in a sample of trapped moles from various parts of Poland, 87–100 per cent of stomachs were largely packed with earthworms in all months (Skoczen, 1966). In contrast, there may be seasonal variations in the importance of earthworms in the diet in other regions; for example, Larkin (1948) working in the English fens found worms in over 90 per cent of stomachs in the winter months but in only 50 per cent during the summer. Such seasonal differences probably result from the fact that earthworms tend to migrate deep into the soil during the hot, dry months of the year, thus becoming less available to moles working nearer to the surface.

Apart from earthworms, the diet of moles consists largely of other soil invertebrates, particularly insect larvae and molluscs. The insects most commonly eaten by the European mole belong to just a few groups, the Elateridae (wireworms), Carabidae (ground beetles and their larvae), Bibionidae (fever fly larvae), Tipulidae (leather-jackets) and Lepidoptera (usually cutworms). However, it is difficult to generalise about diet, as representatives of over 40 families of insects, ranging in size from ants a few millimetres long right up to large carabid beetles, have been found in mole stomachs. It is probably true to say that moles, like most other predatory mammals, are opportunistic and eat what they can get. Thus their stomach contents will reflect pretty accurately what is present in the soil at a given place and time. This has been clearly shown by Oppermann (1968) who carefully sorted through the stomachs of 293 moles caught in a variety of habitats around Berlin. The proportion of

Table 3.2 The biomass of earthworms in different habitats (after Satchell, 1983)

Habitat	kilograms per hectare	
	L. terrestris	Other worms
pasture	673	140
arable	403	67
conifers	0	0.78
birch	130	173

earthworms in the diet varied from less than 10 per cent by volume in moles caught in pinewoods to over 90 per cent in animals from deciduous woodlands. This relates closely to known differences in the invertebrate faunas of different soil types. For example, grassland soils tend to support the greatest biomass of earthworms and the larger arthropods. Among woodlands the rich humic mulls under deciduous forests support much more than the cold, compacted, podzolic soils typical of coniferous forests (Table 3.2). The fauna of these latter soils consists largely of huge numbers of tiny mites and collembola, hardly ideal fare for moles.

In a similarly detailed study, Funmilayo (1979) showed that moles living under grass pastures in south-east Scotland appeared to have no major preferences for particular types of prey. By catching moles and by sorting through samples of soil from the same area he was able to show that they ate what was present and that the proportions of stomachs containing different categories of invertebrates reflected closely the relative abundance of these same groups in the surrounding soil (Figure 3.1).

Figure 3.1 The diet of European moles living in pastures in south-east Scotland (after Funmilayo, 1979)

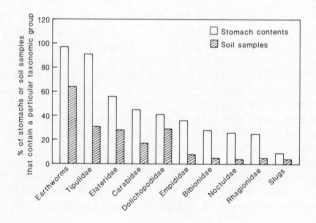

HOW MUCH DO MOLES EAT?

One way to determine how much a mole eats is to trap a sample of animals and to weigh the amount of food in their stomachs. With this information and armed with a knowledge of how frequently stomachs are filled it should be possible to calculate daily intake.

For most of the year, European moles leave their nests three times each day in order to forage (see Chapter 5). A mole's stomach is empty at the beginning of a feeding bout and full when it returns to the nest in order to sleep off its feast. When traps are set in the area, moles will of course be caught at random intervals during a feeding bout and, as a result, almost all will be caught before they have fed to repletion. The problem that arises is how to use the weight of partially filled stomachs to estimate the weight of a full one. One might suggest that the obvious way would be to use the maximum value, but life is not so simple. Figure 3.2 shows the frequency distribution of the weights of the stomach contents of 159 moles from north-east Scotland. The maximum weight recorded was 12.6 g (Godfrey and Crowcroft (1960) give a maximum value of 16 g), but had a larger sample of moles been taken then greater weights than this might well have been encountered. The distribution of weights is clearly asymmetrical and, in fact, corresponds closely to the statistical Poisson distribution. Having calculated the mean weight of food in the stomachs, the Poisson curve can then be used to predict the largest weight that one would be likely to find in a very large sample. The answer turns out to be around 20 g. It seems, therefore, that the average free-living European mole will eat about 60 g of food per day and over the course of a year some 20 kg, of which more than half will usually be earthworms.

Figure 3.2 The frequency distribution of the weights of the stomach contents of moles in north-east Scotland. The smooth curve is the fitted Poisson distribution

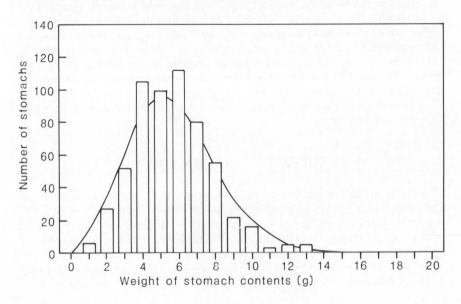

Anyone reading the older literature is likely to be left with the impression that moles are extremely voracious feeders which consume unusually large amounts of food. Thus, a number of authors have made much of the fact that moles daily eat an amount equivalent to 50 per cent or more of their own body-weight (e.g. Mellanby, 1967). At first sight such figures might appear huge, but are they in fact any larger than one would expect?

The average rate at which animals take in food is related to their size and across a wide range of endothermic herbivores and carnivores the relationship is a power function of the form

$$I.R. = 10.7W^{0.70}$$

where I.R. is the average ingestion rate in watts and W the body-weight in kilograms (Farlow, 1976).

We can, of course, use this formula to predict the ingestion rate of an animal of any given size; a 100 g mole for example would be expected to have an average ingestion rate of 2.13 watts, or 184.5 kJ d^{-1}. The earthworm *Lumbricus terrestris*, a particular favourite of moles, has an energy content of 2.947 kJ per gram of living tissue, and thus if a mole were to eat nothing else but earthworms it would need to take in 62.6 g of these creatures per day, which is of course 62.6 per cent of its body weight. It turns out, therefore, that moles are not exceptionally voracious feeders and are, in fact, eating no more than one would expect for any mammal of their size.

Thus far we have dealt with that unusual creature so beloved of statisticians, the 'average animal'. In the real world, of course, different individuals will experience varying energy demands and one would predict that their ingestion rates would vary accordingly. A case in point is the hard-working breeding female. Pregnancy itself is not particularly costly in terms of energy, but during lactation energy demands rise sharply, reaching a peak just before weaning. An inkling of the maternal investment involved can be obtained from the rate at which young moles grow, from 3.5 g at birth to over 60 g at weaning at three weeks of age! In order to cope with this energy burden, nursing moles are forced to increase their food intake. It is noteworthy that it is only during May that stomachs of trapped females tend to contain more food than those of males (Figure 3.3). To meet these increased energy demands, females are forced to increase their total daily foraging time by some 12–15 per cent and to spread it over four feeding bouts each day, instead of the usual three (see Chapter 5).

HOW DO MOLES EAT?

Having discussed what moles eat, we now turn to the question of how they catch their prey. Basically, moles can obtain food in three different ways: by foraging on the surface, by actively digging out prey from the soil, or by gleaning animals that have blundered into the tunnel system.

The star-nosed mole of North America is the only talpid species that regularly forages above ground. This semi-aquatic, semi-fossorial creature spends a significant proportion of each day on the surface, where it

Figure 3.3   The average weights of the stomach contents of male and female European moles at different times of the year

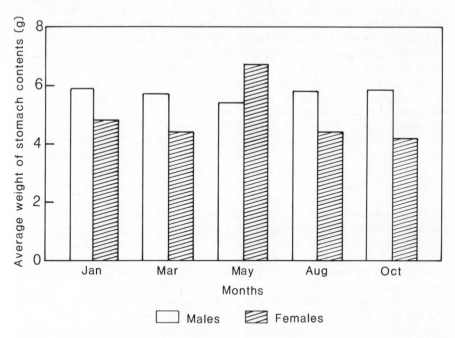

passes the time seeking out aquatic annelids and insects (Yates, 1983). Other species of moles only occasionally leave the comfort of their subterranean strongholds in order to root about among the vegetation. In the case of the European mole, such forays to the surface often take place in the summer, as described in the following extract from a charming letter to the magazine *British Birds* (No. 75, page 90, 1982):

> At 05.15h on 27 August we noticed an erratic movement among leaf litter on the banks of a small dyke ... After a short time the movement among the litter was repeated and we realised it was caused by a mole. A Thrush was feeding among the leafy litter about half a metre from the disturbance ... The mole then surfaced and pushed among the litter, working along the banks of the dyke at considerable speed; it was followed by the Thrush who found invertebrate food among the disturbed litter. After a brief interval the mole disappeared underground ... and then reappeared about 6 m away and the Thrush immediately ran to its new position and began to forage around the disturbance. After 5 or 6 minutes the mole scuttled off through the surface litter, closely followed by the Thrush, and was lost to sight at about 20 m.

Clearly, thrushes find moles rather more useful than humans do!

Apart from instances such as these, talpid moles rarely feed on the surface and emerge from their tunnels only to gather nest materials or when underground life has become pretty intolerable, for example when the ground has become rock hard and arid as a result of prolonged drought (Morris, 1966). Then moles may leave their tunnels to search for food and, probably more importantly, to seek water. Such drouthy quests can be epic in scale; we once followed a radio-tagged mole for over a kilometre until he found a flowing stream. Having drunk his fill he then unerringly retraced his steps before slipping back into his own ground.

For the most part moles obtain their sustenance underground, although the manner in which they do so is a matter of some contention. According to some authors, including Schaerffenberg (1940) and Godet (1951), moles obtain most of their food by actively digging it out of the soil. Mellanby (1967), in contrast, thinks this unlikely and has suggested that the greater part of a mole's dietary intake comes not from the soil itself but from the semi-permanent tunnels which act as 'pit-fall traps' for earthworms and other soil invertebrates. If this is indeed the case then once a tunnel has been dug it acts as a continuing and economic source of food. All that the mole has to do to feed is to systematically trot along its network of tunnels snapping up whatever prey it happens to encounter. While this idea is basically correct, one really must question whether the tunnels actually do act as traps in the strict and proper sense of the word. A denizen of the soil, such as an earthworm, is hardly likely to be 'trapped' by a burrow; what is there to prevent it from leaving the burrow whenever it wishes? A more likely explanation is that soil animals are continuously entering and leaving the tunnel system during the course of their subterranean wanderings and migrations. The animals present in the tunnels at any given time are not in any sense prisoners, trapped until eaten, but rather represent a standing crop of potential prey which is dynamically changing as new individuals enter the tunnels and others leave.

These ideas might seem eminently plausible, but is there hard evidence that prey are to be found in the tunnels and, if so, are the quantities present likely to be adequate to meet a mole's daily requirements? That prey animals do enter the tunnels made by moles is beyond question; both Haeck (1969) and Jensen (1986) have shown that small containers sunk into the floor of a tunnel soon collect a variety of invertebrates including leather-jackets, beetle larvae, centipedes and earthworms. Unfortunately, such methods are largely qualitative and can only tell us what species are present in the tunnels, together with a very crude estimate of the relative abundance of different groups. Haeck has gone on to tackle the more difficult problem of quantifying the absolute amount of prey present, by regularly inspecting stretches of tunnel. In order to expedite these observations the roof was removed from sections of tunnel and replaced with planks of wood which could quickly be whipped aside to reveal any prey animals present at that instant. These observations revealed that the quantity of prey present in the tunnels varied from one time of the day to another and also fluctuated seasonally. However, some clear patterns were evident; earthworms, for example, were much more likely to be present in the tunnels during the hours of darkness than during daylight (Figure 3.4). The quantity of food present in the tunnels appears, at first sight, to be impressive but is it adequate to sustain a mole? Unfortunately, the answer seems to be no! Given the average densities of worms per metre of tunnel shown in Figure 3.4, a mole gleaning along 1,200 m of tunnel per day, a most

Figure 3.4 The weight of worms present in mole tunnels at different times of the day (after Haeck, 1969)

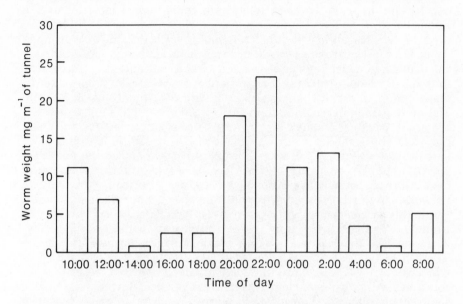

reasonable distance, would be able to collect only about 10 g of earthworms, a quantity far short of its daily requirements. At face value, therefore, the quantities of food in the tunnels would seem to be inadequate to sustain an active mole. However, for a variety of reasons, this need not be the case. To begin with, the roof of the tunnel, a major source of migrating soil animals, had been replaced with lifeless pieces of wood. This structural modification may also have altered the micro-climate of the tunnels, thus making them less acceptable to the creatures of the soil. In addition, any earthworms that happened to be only partially in the tunnel when the artificial roof was removed would have rapidly withdrawn into their own burrows and could have been missed by the human observer, although they would have been snapped up by any adept mole. Finally, an actively foraging mole not only picks up animals from the tunnel floor but also continually probes into the walls with its sensitive snout, and in this way discovers additional prey, prey that are invisible to the human eye.

Before we continue this discussion of feeding biology it is worth digressing for a few moments, in order to look at the senses used by the mole in such probing of the soil column. Talpids have poor visual acuity, and besides they usually feed in the dark, but that weakness is more than compensated for by their acute hearing and by a quite exquisite sense of touch. The snouts of both moles and desmans are tipped with a unique battery of touch-sensitive structures, numbering several thousands and known as Eimer's organs (Quilliam, 1966). Under a powerful lens these manifest themselves as a mass of bulbous protuberances, reminiscent of a cobbled street in miniature (Figure 3.5). In section, and under the microscope, it can be seen that each organ consists of a papilla of

47

Figure 3.5 Scanning electron micrograph of the Eimer's organs on the nose of a European mole (Photo: Martyn L. Gorman)

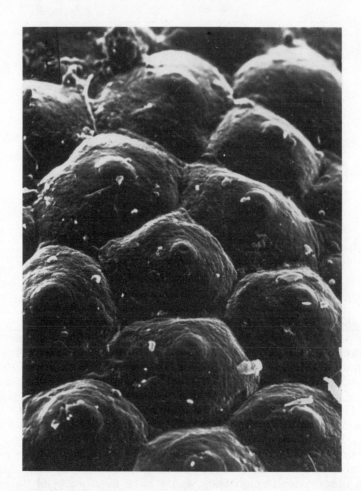

thickened epidermis, which is attached to neighbouring organs by strips of thin, pliable epidermis (Figure 3.6). Each organ is surrounded at its base by large blood-filled sinuses and sits on top of a plexus of sensory nerves. From this plexus a number of bare nerve endings pass up into the thick epidermal cap. When an Eimer's organ is disturbed it is able to rock on its fluid foundations and in this way the stimulus is mechanically transmitted to the nerve endings and on, via the sensory nerves, to the central nervous system. There, the stimuli are integrated with those from any other organs that have been distorted, thus providing information about the nature of the disturbing force. This information can be extremely subtle and rich in detail. The Pyrenean desman, for example, can use its complex of Eimer's organs to detect and to differentiate between minute surface details of objects. This ability has been clearly shown by Richard (1982) who trained a tame desman to decide which of two boxes contained a food reward, using as the only clue a variety of

1. *Rough-haired golden mole from the Transkei (Photo: Anthony Bannister Photo Library)*

2. *Grant's golden mole swimming through the sands of the Namib Desert (Photo: Anthony Bannister Photo Library)*

3. *Star-nosed mole resting on a rock (Photo: Dwight R. Kuhn).*

4. *Star-nosed mole catching a worm at the bottom of a pool (Photo: Dwight R. Kuhn)*

5. *European mole moving through a natural tunnel in the soil* (Photo: Paul Taylor)

6. *European mole breaking the surface on a frosty morning* (Photo: R. David Stone)

7. *Pyrenean desman sitting on a rock (Photo: R. David Stone)*

8. *Pyrenean desman habitat in the French Pyrenees (Photo: R. David Stone)*

9. *Molehills in Northern Scotland (Photo: Martyn L. Gorman)*

10. *Shallow surface tunnels made by a European mole in a newly sown barley field (Photo: Martyn L. Gorman)*

11. A fortress constructed by a European mole in Northern Scotland (Photo: Martyn L. Gorman)

12. A cross-section through a fortress showing the internal tunnels (Photo: R. David Stone)

13. The nest of a European mole (Photo: Martyn L. Gorman)

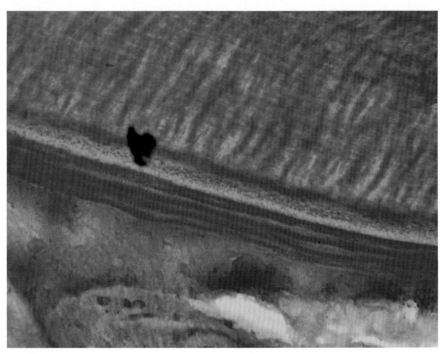

14. A cross-section through the canine tooth of a European mole. The growth rings indicate that the mole was in its fifth year of life. (Photo: Martyn L. Gorman)

15. *A European mole with a radio transmitter glued to its tail* (Photo Martyn L. Gorman)

16. *A dissection of the lower abdomen of a European mole showing the paired preputial scent glands* (Photo: Martyn L. Gorman)

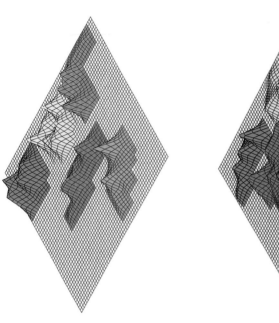

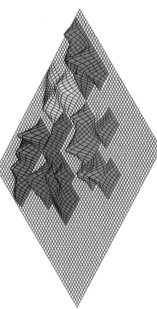

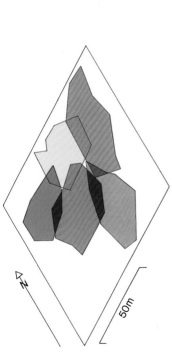

17. The overlapping territories of five neighbouring moles

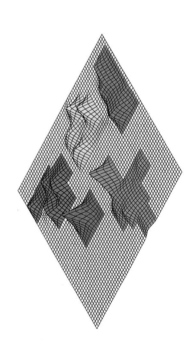

18–20. The areas used by each of the five moles during three consecutive activity periods. The plots were made by dividing the map into a matrix of 25 m² and counting the number of times the moles were located in each. The maps are drawn as if viewed from the south-east with the observation point situated 10,000 map units from the centre of the matrix and 20° above the horizontal. (Produced by Martyn L. Gorman)

Figure 3.6 *Drawing of a cross-section through an Eimer's organ from the snout of a European mole*

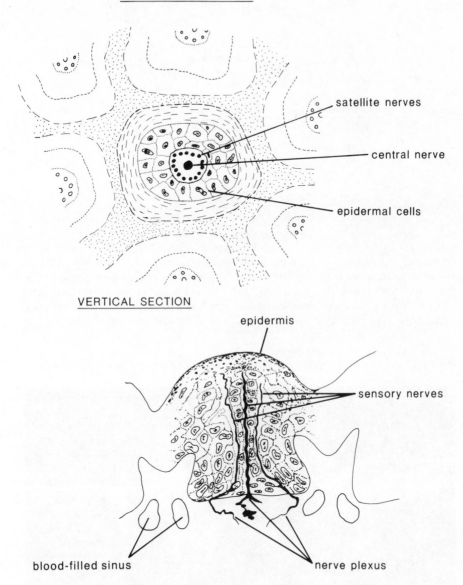

HORIZONTAL SECTION

satellite nerves

central nerve

epidermal cells

VERTICAL SECTION

epidermis

sensory nerves

blood-filled sinus

nerve plexus

textures engraved on their lids (Figure 3.7). By this means he was able to show that the animal is quite capable of detecting, with its Eimer's organs, engraved lines which are only $\frac{1}{15}$ mm in depth and width.

Talpids are also well endowed with sensory hairs or vibrissae. In the European mole these are found on and under the chin, on the muzzle, and in tufts on the sides of the face just behind the ears (Figure 3.8). The

Figure 3.7 A Pyrenean desman successfully opens a container having decided, on the basis of lines engraved on the lid, that it contains food (after Richard, 1982)

backs of the forefeet are also equipped with stout hairs that form outwardly protruding fringes around the palms. Finally, the tail is covered with a mass of sensory hairs (Figure 1.7) but unlike those of the face and feet these do not seem to be directly involved in finding and handling prey. In structure, vibrissae are hairs of large diameter and are relatively rigid so that when displaced they do not bend much, but

Figure 3.8 Sensory vibrissae on the head and forelimbs of a European mole (Photo: Andrew Lucas)

instead act as levers transmitting the applied force to their base. Unlike normal hairs they are embedded in a fluid-filled sac so that they can move about within the skin. When they do so, the mechanical stimulus is amplified and transmitted to the hundreds of nerve receptors of various kinds which lie within the sac. The sophistication of the system is such that the movements of the vibrissae can be analysed in terms of direction, amplitude, velocity and duration of displacement. When all the incoming information from the vibrissae and Eimer's organs is integrated together it is very likely that the mole's world of touch is as rich in detail as the dog's world of smell, and just as incomprehensible to a visually orientated species such as ourselves.

We can now return to the mole foraging in its dark but tactile world. It has long been thought that moles may have an impact on the populations of soil invertebrates on which they feed. In continental Europe, in the days before modern insecticides, cockchafer larvae were a serious pest in orchards and arable crops, and then moles were welcome neighbours. Indeed, Schaerffenberg (1940) records instances of moles being deliberately seeded into such areas, to act as pest-control agents. Whether or not the total biomass of prey in an area where moles are present is reduced compared to similar areas without moles has yet to be determined. However, there is now good evidence that invertebrate populations are somewhat reduced in the immediate vicinity of mole tunnels. Jensen (1986) has shown that, compared to undisturbed soil, prey biomass is reduced by up to 80 per cent in the soil immediately surrounding the relatively shallow tunnels dug by *Parascalops breweri* (Figure 3.9). However, such effects may be very limited in extent; by taking soil samples at given distances from the tunnels of European moles, Haeck (1969) was able to show that the reduction in prey biomass extended for only some 10 cm out into the soil.

There is little doubt, therefore, that the soil fauna around mole tunnels is reduced in density. However, this reduction may not be the result of mole predation — life is never simple! When Jensen excluded moles from particular tunnels by means of exclosures set into the soil, the soil fauna remained depleted for at least three months (Jensen, 1986). In fact, tunnels that had been abandoned by moles for at least a year were still surrounded by areas of depauperate soil. One must conclude from evidence such as this that the observed reductions in soil fauna may not be the result of mole predation. It could simply be that soil invertebrates tend to avoid, to some extent, the soil immediately around mole tunnels because it is rather drier than undisturbed soil.

Whatever the reason, the fact remains that the biomass of invertebrates, and in particular of earthworms, is much reduced in the immediate vicinity of mole tunnels. One must question, therefore, why moles dig permanent tunnels, at great energetic expense, rather than feeding by digging through undisturbed soil near to the surface where food is more abundant. To understand why, it is necessary to look at the relative costs and benefits of each feeding strategy. Jensen (1986) has done just this for *Parascalops breweri*, a species which frequently digs at the surface but which also constructs deeper, semi-permanent tunnels.

As we showed in Chapter 2, the energy costs of digging are high, and this is true even in shallow digging, when the mole merely moves the soil

Figure 3.9 Seasonal changes in the relationship between the density of prey (expressed as energy per litre of soil) in undisturbed soil and in the soil immediately around tunnels made by Parascalops breweri. The straight line shows what the relationship would be if the two types of soil contained similar densities of prey. In reality, the disturbed soil always contains less prey (after Jensen, 1986)

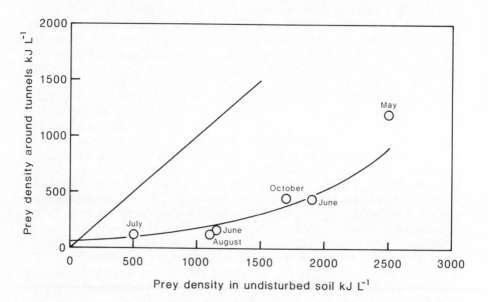

aside rather than pushing it up to the surface to form molehills. Jensen has calculated that for *P. breweri* the cost of digging these surface tunnels, at a speed of 10 m h^{-1}, is about 0.23 kJ m^{-1}. In contrast, the cost of moving through pre-existing tunnels at a speed of 34 m h^{-1} is only of the order of 0.03 kJ m^{-1}. Given these differential costs it does not necessarily follow that a mole will find food more economically by digging in undisturbed areas. The lower gains to be expected from feeding from the depleted soil around the semi-permanent tunnels may be more than offset by the lower costs of locomotion. In order to see if this is the case, it is necessary to estimate the energetic return to be expected from each feeding method. To do so, one needs to know the volume of soil that is searched per metre travelled in the two strategies and the prey content of that soil. The densities of prey in undisturbed soil and in soil around the tunnels are already known and shown in Figure 3.9. Jensen calculated that a mole digging through the surface soil may scan up to 0.948 l of soil for every metre it digs. In the case of foraging through existing tunnels, it was assumed that a mole can effectively probe and search, by sound and touch, to a depth of 10 mm around the tunnel, a volume of 1.41 l of soil per metre of tunnel. (In addition, the mole will also encounter prey actually in the tunnel, but Jensen appears to have ignored this extra source of income.)

Taking these various factors into account, together with the fact that animals use more energy at low ambient temperatures just to keep warm, Jensen was able to calculate how long a mole would need to forage, either

Figure 3.10 The length of time for which a mole must forage each day in order for the benefits gained to equal the costs incurred at different densities of prey. The upper curves are for a mole digging through undisturbed soil at ambient temperatures of 5 and 20°C. The lower curves are for a mole feeding by gleaning prey from existing tunnels at the same two temperatures. Note that a mole can always break even more rapidly by gleaning than by digging, regardless of the density of prey (after Jensen, 1986)

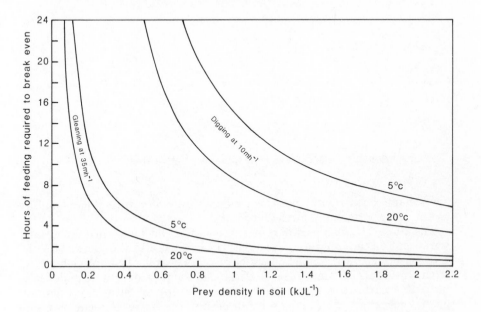

by digging or by gleaning along tunnels, in order to break even, i.e. to gather enough food to balance the expenses of foraging. It turns out that over a wide range of prey densities and ambient temperature a mole can always break even more rapidly by gleaning in existing tunnels than it can by digging through virgin soil (Figure 3.10). In the case of the surface digging strategy, it can only break even within the eight hours normally spent foraging per day at the very highest prey densities. Clearly, therefore, at most prey densities it makes sense for a mole to reuse existing tunnels rather than continually to dig through the surface soil, despite the fact that prey become reduced, for whatever reason, around the permanent tunnels.

Thus, despite the apparent simplicity of their diet, the foraging of moles turns out to be an unexpectedly complex affair that involves them in making difficult economic decisions.

4 Life and death

Until death it is all life. *Don Quixote*, Cervantes

This chapter deals with those two events that every animal can be quite certain of experiencing: birth and death.

The life cycles of the different species of talpid moles are essentially variations on the same simple theme. There is usually one short reproductive season in the spring when males go off in search of receptive females. Apart from this brief but intense stirring of the passions, male moles take no further part in the reproductive process. Having served as many females as they can, they retire to the solitude of their territories to recuperate and to await the arrival of the next spring. The resultant pregnancies last for about 4–5 weeks and lead to the birth of litters numbering 2–8 young. Lactation lasts for about 4–5 weeks, at the end of which time the young leave their mother's nest and start to catch food for themselves. Some days or weeks later the young moles are evicted from their natal territory and go off in search of a home of their own. Those that succeed in establishing themselves in a territory will breed in the following spring, and in each succeeding year until they die.

We can now look at some of these events in rather more detail. Unfortunately there are only snippets of information available for most species and, much of this account will therefore be based on *Talpa europaea* and some of the North American species.

THE BREEDING SEASON

Just precisely when a mole breeds will depend upon where it lives. In most parts of the world it is much better to be born at some times of the year than at others! In a seasonal environment those young animals which are weaned at a time when food is plentiful will have a better chance of survival than young born at other times. Equally, a mother who gives birth when her own food is in good supply will be better able to cope with the energetic onslaught of lactation and will have a better chance of surviving to breed another year. It is not surprising, therefore, to find that most mammals have a more or less restricted breeding season, with mothers giving birth at that time of the year which maximises their production of surviving young. At the higher latitudes of the Northern Hemisphere most species, including the talpids, give birth during the spring or early summer.

It is usually quite easy to guess which environmental pressures have led to the evolution of breeding seasons; what is not so immediately obvious is just how an animal 'knows' that the time to breed has arrived. To make matters even more complicated, the potential parents have to anticipate the arrival of the best season for giving birth; if the young are to be born at the most advantageous time, then the maturation of gametes and fertilisation must take place somewhat earlier.

It is now clear that animals achieve this careful timing by using environmental cues that change seasonally, and in a predictable manner, to initiate their reproductive activities. The most reliable seasonal oscillator is day-length and this is the major cue used to control the timing of breeding by a wide variety of animals, including most mammals. However, environmental conditions vary, both from one year to the next and from locality to locality. Animals surmount this problem by also using a variety of other environmental cues, particularly temperature and food availability, to determine the onset of breeding in any given year. Thus, according to the old mole-catchers, whereas all English moles breed on an increasing day-length in the spring, the exact time of peak breeding is affected by local soil conditions. Populations living in cold clay soils consistently breed a little later than populations in warm sandy soils just a few miles away (Godfrey & Crowcroft, 1960). In effect, day-length acts like the coarse focus of a microscope and the other environmental factors the fine focus.

Because all talpid moles breed at a time of increasing day-length, there is every reason to believe that photoperiod is involved in the timing of their breeding cycles. The eyes of most moles, including *T. europaea*, are small and largely hidden in the fur, but they are fully formed and open to the outside world. One would guess, therefore, that they are capable of detecting light. Recently, Johannesan-Gross (1988) has not only confirmed that this is indeed the case, but has also managed to measure the approximate levels of illumination that moles can detect. In these elegant experiments eight European moles were trapped, tamed, and trained to choose which of the two arms of a Y shaped maze led to a food reward. The only cue on which the moles could base their decision was the relative level of illumination in the two arms, the brighter one being the one with the reward. The results showed that moles can most certainly distinguish between light and dark; six of them were able to make the discrimination when the rewarded side of the maze was illuminated to a brightness of 100 milliLamberts (mL). To put this into some form of perspective one might note that humans can detect a stimulus of 6×10^{-7} mL, whereas owls can visually detect food at an illumination level of 0.8×10^{-7} mL. These are very low levels indeed; the stimulus that can be detected by a human conveys energy to the eye at a rate of only 9×10^{-16} watts, an amount of power that would take 150 million years to raise the temperature of one gram of water by one degree centigrade!

Moles can therefore clearly detect light, but how on earth can a fossorial animal that spends its life underground use day-length to organise its sex life? In fact moles come to the surface more often than one might imagine

(Morris, 1966). Their nests consist of vegetation that has to be collected from the surface, and they occasionally emerge to forage and, in summer, to drink. In addition, moles are without doubt exposed to low levels of light when digging surface tunnels or when pushing spoil to the surface from their deep burrow systems. Consequently, moles are on occasion exposed to light, albeit irregularly, infrequently and at low levels. But that does not in any way preclude the use of light as a signal, since it is now clear that it is not the length of exposure that is important in initiating breeding. What is important is that the light be received at the appropriate time. There is, hidden away in the neuro-endocrine apparatus of all mammals, a receptor system that exhibits a circadian (approximately 24 hour) rhythm of sensitivity to light. The system is sensitive to light only during a relatively short period of time during each 24 hours. However, during this photosensitive phase, even a brief exposure to very dim light can suffice to initiate the series of endocrine events that eventualy leads to gonadal maturation and to reproduction.

Figure 4.1 The timing of breeding at different latitudes for two species of moles. Both species breed progressively later as one moves north. The figure also shows the day-length at which European moles breed at different parts of their distribution

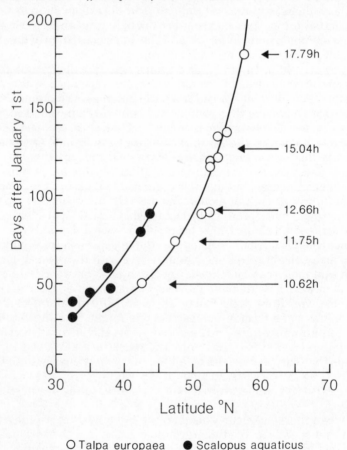

O Talpa europaea　● Scalopus aquaticus

It is the position of this photosensitive phase within the circadian rhythm, relative to the animal's 'dawn', that is open to selection by environmental pressures and which determines at what time of the year an individual will breed. Thus, in those species which breed early in the year, the photosensitive phase lies early in the circadian rhythm, relatively soon after 'dawn'. As a result such animals are stimulated by the short days of spring. In contrast, animals which have evolved to breed in midsummer have a sensitive phase so late in the circadian rhythm that it receives light only during the long days of summer.

Thus it is that different populations of moles breed at different times of the year and at different day-lengths. Take for example *Talpa europaea* which is distributed across Europe, from the Mediterranean northward into Scandinavia (Figure 4.1). In general, populations in the southern part of the species' range breed early in the year, but breeding occurs progressively later as one moves north. Thus the peak time for pregnancies in central Italy is in the second half of February (Balli, 1940) but not until late June in north-east Scotland. These geographical differences in the time of breeding have undoubtedly evolved in response to regional variations in soil temperatures and food availability, both of which peak later in the year at higher latitudes. In order to cope with such regional climatic variations, European moles living at different latitudes have evolved physiological differences in their patterns of sensitivity to light, breeding on a day-length of only ten hours or so in the south but not in the north until day-lengths have reached 17 hours (Figure 4.1).

Sadly, relatively few detailed data are available on the breeding seasons of other species of moles. All seem to breed in the spring and summer, and most show regional variations in the exact time of reproduction. The North American species *Scalopus aquaticus*, for example, behaves like the European mole in that it breeds later in the north than in the south (Figure 4.1). There is also some evidence that the star-nosed mole exhibits latitudinal variation in the time of breeding (Eadie & Hamilton, 1956).

SEASONAL CHANGES IN THE REPRODUCTIVE ORGANS AND SEXUAL BEHAVIOUR

Mole-catchers have long known that all moles are males until they are a year old when they become separated into males and females. (Folklore, quoted in Harrison Matthews, 1935.)

If only that were true, what wonderful opportunities for research would present themselves! The root of the conundrum is that European moles have something in common with spotted hyenas in that the two sexes can be a bit difficult to tell apart. For much of the year the external appearance of the genitals of male and female moles is rather similar, with the female urinary papilla quite closely resembling the penis of the male. To make matters even more difficult, the vagina is usually completely sealed with skin and all but invisible. Only during the breeding season when the vagina becomes perforated are the two sexes obviously different. As Ivy Compton-Burnett said in the novel *Mother and Son*, 'There is more difference within the sexes than between them.' However, those with a burning

Figure 4.2 Seasonal changes in the sexual organs of European moles living in the British Isles. The upper part of the figure shows changes in the weight of the testes and prostate gland; the lower part illustrates changes in the testosterone content of the testes and in numbers of spermatozoa stored in the epididymes (partly after Racey, 1978)

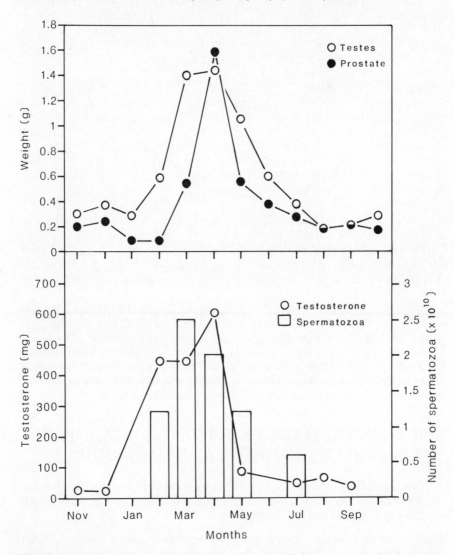

desire to be able to sex moles need not despair! With a careful external examination it is possible to determine the sex of a mole at all times of the year. To begin with, males are generally larger than females and, although there is a degree of overlap in body-weights, one can be pretty sure that an adult weighing more than 100 g will be a male while one weighing less than that is likely to be a female. An even better method of sexing a mole is to measure the distance from the anus to the base of the urinary papilla. In adult males the gap between the two is almost always more than 5 mm whereas in females it is well under 4 mm.

The Male Cycle

The dramatic and seasonal alterations that take place in the external appearance of moles are mirrored by equally impressive changes in the internal organs. The best documented species is the European mole, in which the seasonal changes that take place in the size of the male reproductive organs are quite spectacular (Figure 4.2). On average, the testes are at their smallest in July, following their collapse at the end of that year's breeding attempt. Thereafter they grow slowly until around January when spermatogenesis recommences and then they begin to grow rapidly in size. At the same time the epididymes increase greatly in weight as they become charged with stored and maturing spermatozoa. The timing of peak testis growth and of spermatogenesis varies from locality to locality but generally commences early in the south and later in the north (Figure 4.3). The peak of testis weight and sperm production lasts for only a short period before the testes once again collapse and regress. However, large numbers of fertile spermatozoa remain stored in the epididymes up to three months after the cessation of sperm production. These normally go to waste but occasionally they may be put to use in siring the second litters that are sometimes found. Godfrey (1956), for example, has described some females caught in the fens of East Anglia as being in oestrus during late October, while late litters have been reported in England in September (Barrett-Hamilton, 1910) and in Germany as late as October (Becker, 1959).

Testis growth and spermatogenesis are associated with increased levels of prduction of the male sex hormone testosterone (Racey, 1978). It is against this background of elevated hormone levels that male moles begin to seek out receptive females. For the greater part of the year all moles remain steadfastly within the confines of their individual territories (see

Figure 4.3 Geographical variation in the timing of peak testis weight in European moles

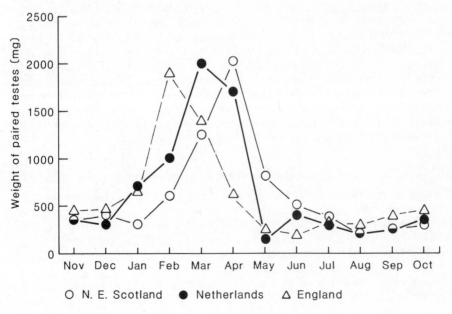

Chapter 6). However, in February and March, as the sap and animal passions begin to rise, males begin to make exploratory excursions outside their normal ranges. Sometimes they do so above ground, but more usually they dig long, straight tunnels, which extend radially from their own territory, until they sense and break into the tunnel system of an attractive and welcoming female. Precisely how they recognise a female who is likely to be amorous rather than greet them with the more usual frenzied attack is unknown. However, it is very likely that female moles, in common with most other mammals, signal their readiness to mate by means of odorous chemicals excreted in their urine. Given their diet of earthworms, which contain some 98 per cent water, moles must urinate a great deal and it is likely therefore that the tunnel system becomes liberally anointed with this olfactory medium.

Male moles invest a great deal of energy and time in finding potential partners; after all, biologically speaking, this is their only *raison d'être*. During the few weeks, or even days, that are available for mating the daily pattern of activity of the males changes dramatically as they frenetically dig and search. Normally they would regularly return to their nests in order to sleep, but at this time they continue to dig until exhausted and then they merely snatch 'cat-naps' in the tunnels, before returning to their labours. During this short period of the year their only thought is to find, and to mate with, as many females as possible. The proportion of males that actually succeed in mating is completely unknown; we have no idea as to the degree of competition amongst males for females nor what factors determine the success of any particular individual. For example, while it is known that males are potentially capable of breeding when they are almost a year old, we do not know if all manage to do so, or whether their chances of mating are in any way dependent upon age and experience. Equally unknown is what role, if any, the female plays in mate choice.

The act of copulation almost always takes place in the privacy of the tunnels, well away from the prying eyes of humans. Arthur Randall, who was a professional mole-catcher in England, witnessed moles mating above ground on only three occasions, despite 70 years devoted to their study (Mellanby, 1971). From what he observed, the mating of moles appears to be in no way unusual. Despite all the effort that goes into bringing it about, the relationship between male and female seems to be a fleeting one. For example, A.J.B. Rudge recounts how a male which he was tracking by means of a radioactive tail ring, found a willing female, entered her nest, consorted with her for about an hour and then departed, presumably in search of further partners (Mellanby, 1971).

The Female Cycle

Female moles, like males, are capable of breeding when they are almost one year old and most do. A particularly fascinating and unusual feature of the female reproductive cycle involves the ovaries, which are quite unlike those of other mammals (Matthews, 1935; Deansley, 1966). From birth onwards each ovary consists of two distinct parts which are known as the follicular and medullary ovaries. The follicles which give rise to the eggs are concentrated in a small crescent of tissue which sits, like a cap, on the much larger mass of the medullary ovary. There is no doubt that the medullary tissue is endocrine in nature and involved in the synthesis of hormones, but what hormones and to what purpose is as yet unknown. One possibility is that for most of the year the medullary tissue produces male hormones and that these are responsible for the aggressive nature of the female and for the masculine appearance of her external genitalia.

From the end of one breeding season until the following spring the follicular tissue is relatively quiescent, while the medullary portion of the ovary is enlarged and clearly active. During this time the uterus is small and flaccid and the vagina is sealed off. All this changes with the beginning of the breeding season when the medullary part of the ovary shrinks and a number of follicles begin to develop and mature. The vagina perforates, the uterus enlarges and the female comes into oestrus, or heat, probably only for some 24–36 hours, and then she ovulates. Whether or not the mole is an induced ovulator, with the eggs being released only after the stimulation of copulation is unknown, but the high pregnancy rate suggests strongly that it is. Thanks to the Herculean digging efforts of the males very few females go unnoticed and it is unusual to find females who are neither pregnant nor lactating in the summer months.

The length of gestation is not known with complete accuracy for any species of mole, but is probably of the order of four weeks in most cases. Most of the available data on the numbers of offspring that are produced by moles have come from the dissection of trapped animals. The number of embryos ranges from two to eight but again the data are fragmentary apart from the European mole and a few North American species. In the case of *Talpa europaea* mean litter sizes vary from one locality to another, generally being smallest in the United Kingdom and increasing as one goes east or south (Table 4.1). The number of young that actually end up being born will be somewhat less than these embryo counts, due to prenatal mortality, which ranges widely from as little as 2–3 per cent (Godfrey, 1956; Haeck, 1969) up to 25 per cent (Morris, 1961). A major cause of embryo resorption is very likely to be food shortage and the

Table 4.1 Litter sizes of *T. europaea*

Location	Mean Litter Size	Author
England	3.63±0.1	Adams (1903)
England	3.80±0.11	Larkin (1948)
England	3.82±0.13	Godfrey (1956)
England	3.90	Morris (1961)
Scotland	3.5 ±0.11	Gorman & Stone (in press)
Holland	4.6 ±0.23	Haeck (1969)
Germany	4.02±0.09	Haeck (1969)
Italy	4.87±0.12	Balli (1940)
Poland	5.12±0.22	Stein (1953)
Urals	5.08±0.39	Bashkirov & Zharkov (1934)
Ukraine	5.73±0.06	Milyutin (1941)

Figure 4.4 The pattern of growth in European moles during their first month of life (after Godfrey & Crowcroft, 1960)

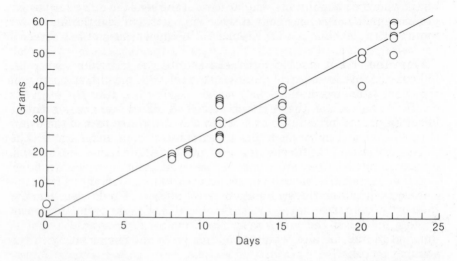

unpredictability of this factor probably explains the wide variations in rates of embryo loss from year to year, and from one place to another.

Following their birth the young are suckled in the nest for about four or five weeks. Newly born moles are blind, hairless, and bright red in colour. However, within a few days they have turned a healthy shade of pink and by the ninth day they have taken on a bluish tinge as the fur begins to form. By the fourteenth day the fur is beginning to erupt from the skin and by day 17 the coat is complete. Finally, on day 22 the eyes open and the young moles get their first glimpse of darkness. The growth of young moles is quite phenomenal and testifies to the quality of their mother's milk. Newly born, they weigh around 3.5 g but by the age of three weeks they weigh nigh on 60 g (Figure 4.4). A human baby growing at the same rate would reach 112 lb before it was a month old!

Very little is known about the number of young moles that die in their nest prior to weaning. Foxes sometimes dig out nests and then, of course, the whole litter is likely to be lost. In the New World the rubber boa, *Charina bottae*, is reported to be a major predator of nestling coast moles (Maser *et al.*, 1981). Other young suffer less violent ends; for example, of 50 litters dug up by Godfrey (1956), three contained one dead youngster and in six all had died. Without doubt, such losses in the nest are most often related to periods of food shortage, and as a result they will vary considerably in magnitude from place to place and from one year to the next.

FINDING A HOME

Since moles are essentially solitary creatures, tolerant of each other's company only for that minimal contact necessary for procreation, it follows that young animals must at some stage leave their mother's territory to seek out a range of their own. Leaving home, or natal dispersal as it is more properly termed, can be centrally important in the adjustment of population sizes to the available food supply. Just how important it can be, has been clearly demonstrated in experiments with microtine voles (Boonstra & Krebs, 1977). When these workers fenced off areas of ground, thus physically preventing the dispersal of young voles away from their area of birth, the number of individuals increased markedly until eventually they overate their food supply, at which point the population crashed.

The behaviour of newly weaned moles is difficult to observe but has been studied in some detail by Godfrey (1957a), who attached radioactive rings to the tails of two mothers and to three of their offspring. With the help of a Geiger counter she was then able to follow the movements of the animals for about ten weeks after weaning. All three youngsters, a male and two females, behaved in a similar way, first venturing out from their maternal nests when they were around 34 days old. These first excursions were very tentative in nature, the moles exploring for only a few metres before they returned to the security of the nest. However, they quickly gained confidence and within five days were making extensive travels along their mother's network of tunnels. The two individuals from the same litter appeared to travel together during this time and, on one occasion at least, Godfrey was convinced that they were foraging in the company of their mother.

Eventually, however, the social temperature rises and the young are evicted from their birthplace. The three tagged juveniles remained within the confines of their mothers' territories for at least ten weeks (28 May–12 August) before they dispersed in search of territory of their own. However, post-weaning residence of this length is probably unusual, and elsewhere Godfrey (1957b) states that most young moles start to dig their own systems of tunnels in late May, immediately after weaning. Such differences in the timing of dispersal could, Godfrey argues, reflect the amount of food available in the maternal territory, with the young being chased out early in lean years, but tolerated for longer in years of relative plenty.

Unmolested populations of moles are relatively stable in numbers from year to year and consequently not all dispersing juveniles will succeed in their quest for an empty territory. With an average litter size of around four, and given the very short breeding season, local populations of moles treble in size over a short period, for example from May to June. Some two-thirds of these animals will have disappeared by the next breeding season, either by death or by emigration. It is the young of the year that do the emigrating, and consequently much of the dying.

When young moles disperse they tend to do so above ground or even, when the occasion demands, across open water. It was by this latter route that moles colonised the newly created Oostelijk Flavoland Polder which at its nearest point is some 600 m distant from mainland Holland (Haeck, 1969). During the time when they are dispersing, moles are terribly vulnerable to predation by a variety of birds and mammals, and to being run over by vehicular traffic. An examination of the food of owls and other birds of prey can, therefore, provide evidence as to just when moles disperse as well as information on the ages of the individuals involved.

Figure 4.5 Moles living in southern England are most likely to be taken by tawny owls in July–August (data from Southern, 1954)

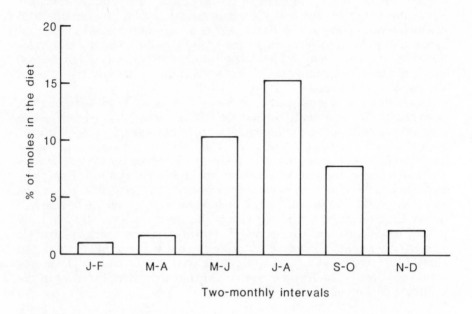

For most of the year, predators take moles only occasionally, grabbing them in an opportunistic fashion if they are rash enough to venture forth in search of bedding or to feed on the surface. However, the picture changes considerably in the spring or summer, the precise timing depending upon the locality in question. At these times moles begin to be taken in very much greater numbers. For example, moles account for over 15 per cent of the vertebrates taken by tawny owls (*Strix aluco*) in southern England in July (Figure 4.5, Southern, 1954). In a similar study of the New World barn owl, *Tyto alba*, Giger (1965) found most remains of the coast mole during the summer months. Data such as these suggest that dispersal takes place during the summer, but the picture is painted with a broad brush. Haeck (1969) has added the fine detail by appealing to the public for information on any dead moles that they might have found on the roads of Holland. Collation of the reports revealed the existence of quite a short dispersal period with a peak in traffic fatalities between the middle of June and the middle of July (Figure 4.6).

Measurements of the degree of tooth wear (see below) in these victims of tooth, claw and wheel, indicate that the vast majority are newly weaned individuals. For example, in a European study of buzzard (*Buteo buteo*) ecology, 86.4 per cent of the moles fed to nestlings were juveniles. This is a much higher value than one would expect, given that juveniles account for only an estimated 67 per cent (4/6) of the population at that time of the year.

In case you are feeling sorry for these young moles, consider the following abstract from a note to the journal *Scottish Birds*, entitled 'Mole kills Herring Gull' (Lyster, 1972).

Figure 4.6 The seasonal pattern of road casualties of European moles in Holland (after Haeck, 1969)

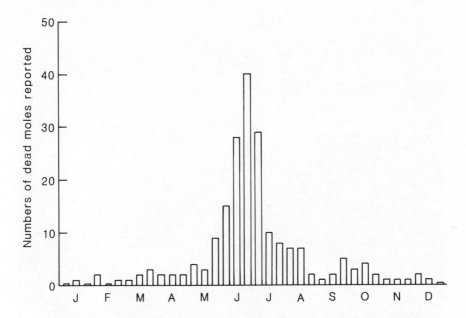

On 12th July 1972 R. Mack found a freshly dead Herring Gull lying in a field ... Protruding from the angle between the neck and left wing was the head of a dead mole. The bodies were sent to the Royal Scottish Museum for a more detailed study.

The conclusions were as follows: the mole had been swallowed alive and probably undamaged. As it was swallowed it had made a 2 cm tear in the top of the gull's oesophagus; from the oesophagus it had passed into the thoracic cavity and into the highly distensible crop-like stomach. The mole then tore through the stomach wall, forced its way through the arch of the furculum (wish-bone) until it came to rest, as discovered, with its head and forelimbs outside the body of the gull. Smears of blood on the gull's neck-feathers suggest that the gull was still alive at this point, though it must have soon succumbed because of the severe damage to the lungs and blood vessels around the heart.

... It would appear that the mole died of suffocation, coupled with exhaustion and shock.

The scene of carnage is depicted in Figure 4.7. Despite such Pyrrhic victories, the number of moles present in a population begin to decrease from May/June onwards, due partly to adult mortality, but mainly because of the demise of young animals. By September the young of the year will either be dead or they will be safely established in a territory of their own. Just how far young moles will have to travel in search of unoccupied but acceptable terrain will depend most of all on the size of the local mole population. In densely populated areas they will have to travel far and

Figure 4.7 *The result of eating a live mole! (Photo: Royal Museum of Scotland)*

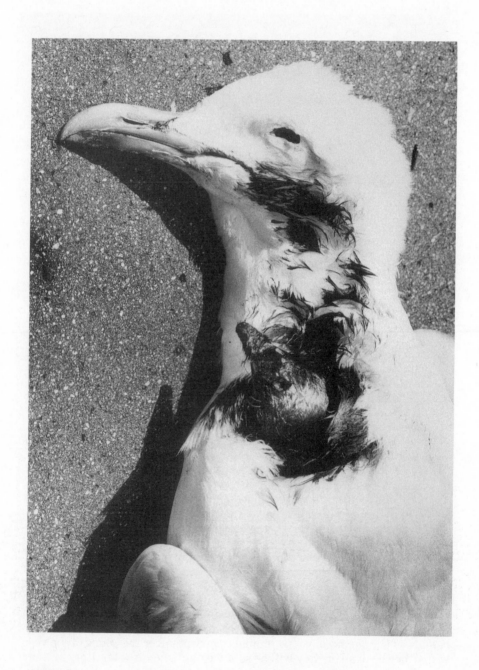

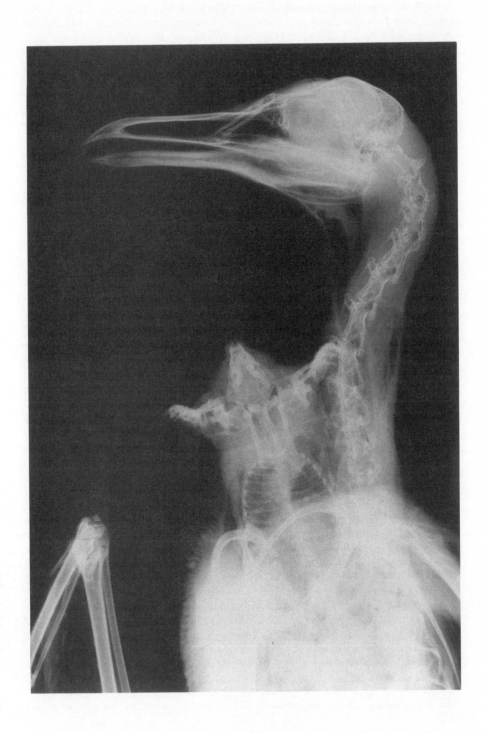

many will be killed, or die of starvation, in the process. Those lucky enough to be born in areas where the resident population is thin on the ground, as a result of recent trapping or natural mortality, will be able to find a vacant patch relatively easily. The result of this is that local populations may differ considerably in their age structures, particularly with regard to the proportion of young animals that they contain. Thus, Larkin (1948) found that a sample of moles from an area that had not been trapped for many years contained only 48 per cent juvenile animals, whereas 96 per cent of those caught in an area that had been trapped out during the previous winter were under one year old. All the evidence therefore points to the fact that it is young moles that disperse in search of unoccupied ground. Once an individual has acquired a territory it will normally continue to live there for the rest of its life, moving little, apart from any minor boundary changes resulting from changes in soil conditions, food availability, or the demise or arrival of neighbours (see Chapter 6).

LIFE EXPECTANCY

How long can a mole expect to live? In order to answer this question one needs to be able to estimate the ages of the moles living in a population. One way of doing so, much used in the past but now largely superseded, was to measure the height of the cheek teeth which, due to the mole's earthy diet, gradually wear away. As we have seen, young moles are added to the population as a sharp pulse once a year. As a consequence, each cohort of moles differs from the next by a full twelve months of tooth wear. When the heights of the molars from a sample of moles are plotted as a frequency histogram they often show a number of peaks, which may represent different age classes. A number of authors have managed to distinguish three classes of tooth wear and on that basis have concluded that moles rarely live beyond three years of age (Larkin, 1948; Stein, 1950; Godfrey & Crowcroft, 1960). Unfortunately, there are serious problems in interpreting data of this kind. To begin with, the teeth of different individuals wear at varying rates, particularly if they are living in soils of different degrees of abrasiveness. The result is that the classes of tooth wear become blurred and difficult to differentiate in any objective manner. This is not a particularly serious problem in the younger age classes which contain relatively large numbers of individuals, but it becomes increasingly acute in the older age groups where fewer and fewer animals are left alive.

Happily, in recent years a more powerful method of determining the ages of mammals has become available. If one makes histological sections through the jaws and teeth of a species such as the mole, it is possible under the microscope to recognise dense growth lines in the bone and in the cementum surrounding the teeth (Plate 14). It is now clear that these lines, like the rings of a tree, are deposited annually and can thus be used to determine the age of the individual (Klevezal & Kleinenberg, 1967; Grue & Jensen, 1979). In the case of the European mole the growth lines are deposited in late winter or early spring, the first one appearing towards the end of the animal's first year of life. When Lodal and Grue

Table 4.2 Life table based on the age distribution (in years) of a mole population trapped in south-west Jutland in September–October 1976. See text for further details (after Lodal & Grue, 1985)

Age	N_x	1_x	d_x	q_x	e_x
0–1	70	1,000	642	0.642	1.17
1–2	20	358	183	0.511	1.38
2–3	11	175	101	0.577	1.30
3–4	4	74	37	0.500	1.39
4–5	1	37	9	0.243	1.27
5–6	3	28	28	1.000	0.50

(1985) applied this technique to a large sample (426) from Denmark, it became apparent that moles can live for much longer than had previously been thought. No less than 44 (10.3 per cent) of the animals in the sample were older than three years of age and one individual was a veritable patriarch in his seventh year of life.

With this accurate method of ageing one can do far more than merely determine the longevity of moles; for example, it is now possible to determine the age at which moles are most likely to die. To do this what is needed is a 'snapshot' of the age structure of a population living in a given place at a given point in time. Of the 426 moles in the sample from Denmark, 109 had been caught in south-west Jutland during a few weeks in the autumn, and from these individuals Lodal and Grue were able to construct a static life table (Table 4.2). Life tables were originally developed by insurance companies which, of course, have a strong vested interest in knowing for how much longer an average human of a given age and sex is likely to be with us. Population biologists are interested in the same sorts of questions but for different reasons, and make wide use of these data structures. Usually, a life table presents survivorship data in several ways so as to permit different kinds of questions about a population to be answered and to predict how it might change in the future.

From the numbers of animals (N_x) of different ages in a sample it is possible to calculate all the other columns or parameters of the life table (Table 4.2). These are:

1_x — the proportion of the original animals that are still alive at the beginning of a particular age interval, x; for example the interval 1–2 years of age. The starting proportion is usually scaled up from 1 to 1,000 in order to standardise presentation and to allow easy comparisons between different populations.

d_x — the number of individuals dying (out of the original 1,000 born) during a particular age interval x.

q_x — the proportion of the survivors alive at the beginning of the interval x which die during that interval.

e_x — the average expectation of further life for an individual alive at the beginning of an age interval.

Figure 4.8 The pattern of mortality suffered by European moles. The figure shows the average number of moles, out of an initial cohort of 1,000, that are still alive in subsequent years (data from Lodal & Grue, 1985)

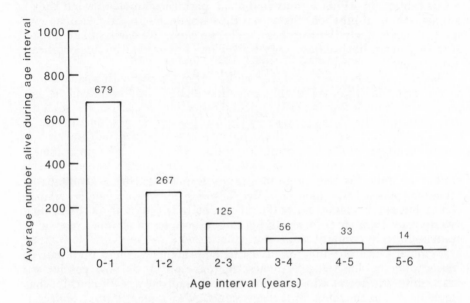

One of the most useful things that can be done with the data in a life table is to plot the number of individuals alive at each age interval (1_x) against age intervals, in what is known as a survivorship curve. If this is done for the Danish moles it is readily apparent that the pattern of mortality in moles is quite different from that of human beings (Figure 4.8). Human beings have a good chance of living long enough to die of old age, surrounded by their children and grandchildren. In other words, our chance of dying is relatively small until we reach old age, but then the chance increases dramatically. Moles, on the other hand, have much the same chance of dying in the coming year whatever their current age. In fact, about 50 per cent of the moles alive at the beginning of any particular age interval will die during the course of the next year, and any mole can expect to live for about a further 1.3 years, regardless of how old it might be at present. The rate of mortality of moles is almost completely independent of age. The exception is during their first year of life. Because of the increased dangers that these young moles face whilst looking for a home, they suffer a rather higher rate of mortality, at around 65 per cent, with most deaths occurring during the dispersal phase. The apparent decrease in the rate of mortality in the fifth year of life is probably a sampling artefact due to the very small numbers of animals of that age that are still alive, and is probably of no biological significance.

The pattern of survival depicted in Figure 4.8 will not apply to all mole populations since their age structures will vary, according to their past histories. Thus, in a population subject only to 'natural mortality', yearlings will account for about 50 per cent of the individuals in the population, whereas in areas which have been recolonised following extensive trapping young animals may account for 90 per cent or more of the population.

Life tables can tell us a great deal about patterns of mortality but they tell us nothing at all about the actual causes of death. In the case of a few species, particularly the European mole, we can quite easily make a list of these causes, but we have very little idea of their relative importance in the overall pattern of mortality.

We have already mentioned that moles suffer severe tooth wear owing to the grit that they inevitably consume along with their food. It is conceivable that a few avoid the pit-falls and dangers of life for such a long time that they 'reach the sorry state of having to chew earthworms with their gums', and eventually die of starvation (Godfrey & Crowcroft, 1960). However, given an annual mortality rate of 50 per cent a mole reaching such a venerable age would be fortunate indeed. Most undoubtedly die for other reasons long before their teeth start to give them trouble.

As mentioned earlier, a significant proportion of juveniles die during the dispersal phase of their lives, either because they are eaten or because they succumb to starvation before they have managed to find a new home. Once they have successfully established themselves in a territory moles are relatively safe from predators, but by no means completely so. The remains of adult moles have been recovered from the faeces or stomachs of a wide variety of predators, including birds of prey, storks, herons, crows, foxes, dogs, weasels, stoats, badgers, mink and domestic cats. Most adults are probably taken either when they come to the surface to forage and to collect bedding, or when they are digging shallow tunnels, just beneath the surface of the soil. However, they are not totally secure even when deep underground; Godfrey and Crowcroft (1960) reported how on one occasion, whilst digging out mole nests, they heard a whole family of weasels calling and moving about in the mole tunnels beneath their feet! Any mole stumbling into a band of killers like those would have a pretty hard time of it!

Extreme weather conditions can also affect rates of mortality, either directly or indirectly. During prolonged periods of drought or freezing temperatures most soil invertebrates become immobilised and then moles, unable to dig through the rock-hard soil, can die of starvation in significant numbers (Kirikov, 1946; Lichatschew, 1950). To make matters even worse, during freezing weather, and also during flooding, moles are forced to the surface where they become exposed to the usual battery of predators.

THE IMPACT OF MAN
ON POPULATIONS OF MOLES

Despite the vagaries and undoubted dangers of life, populations of moles do not vary enormously in size from year to year. They do not increase in number without limit, nor do they decline to extinction. Instead, like most animal populations, they tend to fluctuate, but only within a fairly narrow range, around an average level determined by the productivity of the area in which they happen to be living. Following a catastrophe such as flooding or an epidemic, a depleted population tends to return to its 'normal' average density. Equally, if a population rises to an unusually high level in response to a temporary improvement in, let us say, the food supply, it soon returns to its more usual density once the times of plenty come to an end. These homeostatic, or self-regulatory, changes in population size are brought about by density-dependent changes in mortality and/or reproductive output. By density-dependent changes it is meant that rates of mortality increase progressively as population density increases, and conversely that they progressively decrease as it declines.

Fossorial mammals such as moles live in a world that is, on the whole, dependable and relatively unchanging. As a result, year-to-year fluctuations in population size are neither as common nor as as extreme as those suffered by small surface-dwelling mammals. The only agent of change that is likely to bring about a large-scale and rapid decline in the number of moles living in an area is the human mole-catcher.

Today, moles, when they are noticed at all, are usually regarded as pests, but this has not always been the case. In the past they were sometimes seen as beneficial consumers of insect pests and for many years their skins provided a valuable source of income to hard-pressed country folk.

Nowadays, moles are killed, by trapping or poisoning, only when they are thought to be doing damage to agriculture, or causing havoc on the golf course or in the garden. Otherwise, they are largely left alone. At the turn of the century things were very different, with a veritable army of professional mole-catchers dedicated to killing and skinning huge numbers of moles right across Europe and Russia. Moleskins, with their short resilient fur, had been used for clothing for millennia but towards the end of the nineteenth century the fur suddenly became highly fashionable, with the result that demand sky-rocketed. By 1905 over a million skins were being traded annually on the London market alone. The demand for skins was such that mole populations were severely reduced across large tracts of Europe. In Germany fears were expressed for the very survival of the species and applications were made for its protection by the State (Heck, 1912). The industry inevitably declined with the outbreak of the First World War, but recovered with the cessation of hostilities, and underwent a second boom in the early 1920s. At that time over twelve million skins a year were crossing the Atlantic to the USA, 50 per cent of them from Germany alone. Since those heady days, however, the market has progressively declined and today it is practically non-existent. We have heard it claimed that a major cause of the collapse of the market in moleskins was the increase in the number of motor cars. It seems that the problem with moleskin coats is that when they are sat upon for long periods they tend to develop pressure marks that portray all too clearly the finer anatomical details of the wearer. Such is the fickle nature of the world of fashion.

This persecution of moles occurred a long time ago, but with the aid of computer modelling, we can look back into the past to get an idea of what impact such levels of exploitation must have had on local populations. The results of such a modelling exercise are shown in Figure 4.9. The upper part of the figure shows how a population starting with the age

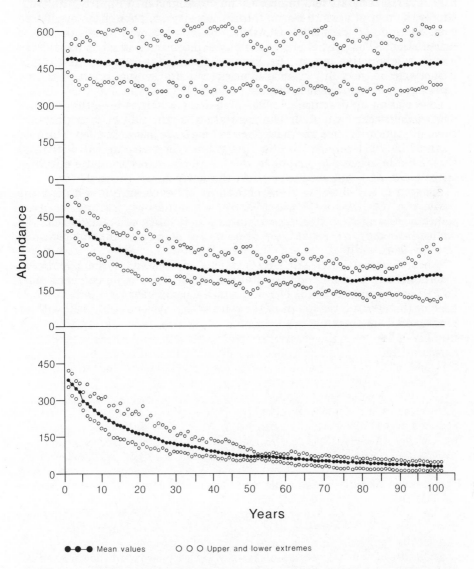

Figure 4.9 Computer simulations of the impact of trapping on mole populations. The figures show predictions of how a population is likely to change over a number of years. In the upper figure the population suffers only natural mortality but in the lower ones an additional 5 or 10 per cent of the animals in each age class are removed annually by trapping

●—●—● Mean values   O O O Upper and lower extremes

structure shown in Figure 4.8, and subject only to the rates of natural mortality shown in Table 4.2, is likely to fluctuate in size through time. The model basically assumes that all the females in the population give birth to 3.5 young when they are twelve months old and in subsequent years for as long as they live. In fact, the situation is a little more complex than this in that reproduction is made density-dependent so that an unexploited population will remain relatively constant in size. In addition, in order to make the model as realistic as possible, the precise

73

rates of mortality and reproduction in the different age classes are varied from year to year in a random manner, but within narrow limits. In this way the model mimics the vagaries of food, climate, predation and disease faced by all real animals. The upper graph in Figure 4.9 shows, for a number of years into the future, the average population size based on 200 runs of the model, together with the extreme upper and lower predictions. The predictions of the model mimic closely what happens in real mole populations; in the absence of exploitation they vary in size from year to year in response to environmental changes, but over long periods their average size remains relatively constant.

Let us now assume that a mole-catcher arrives in an area that had not previously been exploited. The population is still subject to the natural rates of mortality and reproduction that we have just described. The only thing that has changed is that the trapper is going to kill additional moles. The lower two graphs in the figure show the dramatic effects of two different levels of cropping. At the lower level, the mole-catcher is assumed to kill 5 per cent of the animals in each age-class during the course of each year. The second trapper is harder working, or more skilful, and manages to take 10 per cent. It must be stressed that the moles killed by the trappers are over and above the animals that continue to die from natural causes. The figures show that even relatively low levels of exploitation can cause marked decreases in the population density, and give an indication of the impact that mole-catchers must have had over huge areas of Europe in the early years of the century. It says much for the resilience of the species that it is not only still with us but positively thriving.

5 Patterns of activity

If they are to avoid leading a completely frenetic existence, moles, like all other animals, must organise their complex lives, allocating time as necessary to sleeping, feeding, digging, mating and all those other activities that make life worth living. This chapter deals with what little is known about the ways in which moles set about this task, of how they budget their time at different periods of the day and night and at different seasons of the year. Obtaining this kind of information for free-living fossorial animals has proved to be a difficult task and inevitably it has involved the use of some quite complex and specialised techniques.

The first problem is how to catch moles alive and in good health so that they can be individually marked in some way or other. The easiest way is to turn them out with a spade when they are seen to be digging a superficial tunnel just beneath the surface. To catch a mole in a deep burrow is a much more difficult task and requires some kind of live-trap. The most efficient design is the Dutch or Friesian tunnel trap (Figure 5.1). The main part of the trap consists of a block of wood, preferably a hard wood which will not warp or swell when it becomes wet. A hole of the same diameter as a mole tunnel, say 5.5–6.5 cm, is bored through the length of the wooden block. This passage can be closed off at each end by vertical and weighted portcullis doors which, when released, descend into a pair of slots cut into the wood. These doors are best made of perspex or some other rigid and inert plastic. When a mole enters the trap it passes unhindered until it reaches the midpoint of the passage. At that point it bumps into a trigger mechanism which causes the raised doors to drop, thus confining the mole. The prisoner will remain in better condition if a second passage is cut, at right angles to the main passage, allowing access to a nest box filled with hay and victualled with food such as earthworms or blowfly maggots. Friesian traps are not easy to set and require some practice. One must first of all find a suitably straight mole tunnel, and then remove a section the same length as the trap. The trap is then placed in position with very great care so that the holes at each end are aligned accurately with the cut ends of the burrow. The trap must then be inspected on a regular basis, at least once every four hours, if the mole is not to die of cold, wet or stress.

Figure 5.1 A trap for catching moles alive: the Friesian trap

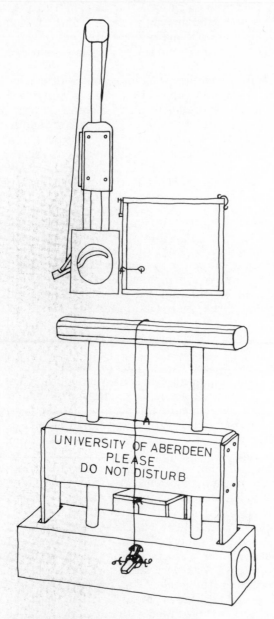

However, catching the mole is just the first of the problems to be overcome. The next is how to follow the mole once it is released. The first real breakthrough in studying the behaviour of unrestrained wild moles was made in the 1950s by Gillian Godfrey, who used radioactive isotopes to monitor the movements and patterns of activity of European moles (Godfrey 1955, 1957a). She did so by soldering metal capsules, containing 80–100 µCi of ^{60}Cobalt, to monel rings (bands) which she then fastened around the narrow bases of the moles' tails. The gamma radiation emitted by this isotope is so intense that it penetrates through the soil and can readily be detected above the ground with the aid of a suitable Geiger counter. In this way Godfrey was able not only to locate tagged moles but also to follow their movements as they went about their daily business.

These early studies, together with later contributions by Haeck (1969) and by Woods & Mead-Briggs (1978), have provided a wealth of interesting and useful data, but it must be admitted that the technique suffers from serious problems of safety. The levels of radiation required to penetrate through the soil are quite high and thus present a fairly serious health risk to the unfortunate mole. In addition, there is always the worry that the mole under study will be taken by the neighbourhood cat, later to be deposited on someone's kitchen floor! Quite apart from questions of safety, the technique also suffers from the fact that the isotope can usually only be detected from a distance of half a metre or less, which means that the mole can be difficult to find at the start of the day's work. Finally, as if these problems were not enough in themselves, only one mole can be tracked in a given area at any one time since the signals emitted by each radioactive ring are to all intents and purposes identical.

These problems have largely been overcome, in our own studies, by substituting miniature VHF radio transmitters for the radioactive rings. The only major problem we faced in developing this technique for moles was attaching the radios in the first place. The time-honoured way would have been to attach them to a collar but unfortunately moles are extremely badly designed in this respect, totally lacking any semblance of a neck. After much thought, we eventually hit on the idea of gluing the radios to the upper surface of the tail, a method which has proved to be most successful (Plate 15). The radios weigh less than 1.5 g and are thus easily carried, even by newly weaned individuals. When operating they emit a short pulse of radio energy several times per second and continue to transmit for several weeks before their batteries expire. The frequencies used by the radios, around 173.2 MHz, readily pass through the soil, and the signals are so powerful that they can be picked up from a distance of several tens of metres. Thus, with the aid of a radio receiver fitted with a directional antenna, a radio-tagged mole can quickly be detected from afar and its position pinpointed to an accuracy of $\pm$ 0.25 m or better. A major advantage of radio-telemetry over the use of isotopes is that each radio transmits on a different frequency so that several moles can be tracked simultaneously in the same piece of ground.

THE DAILY GRIND

Anyone reading Chapter 2 on digging may be forgiven for thinking that moles must be heavily into the work ethic. In fact, the results of some painstaking studies carried out in the Netherlands by Haeck (1969) suggest that this is not the case. Whilst following the movements of 19 moles, each fitted with a radioactive tail ring, Haeck kept careful records of the activities each animal was currently involved in. The moles being

Figure 5.2 The length of time devoted to various activities by European moles at different seasons, together with the average distance travelled per day (after Haeck, 1969)

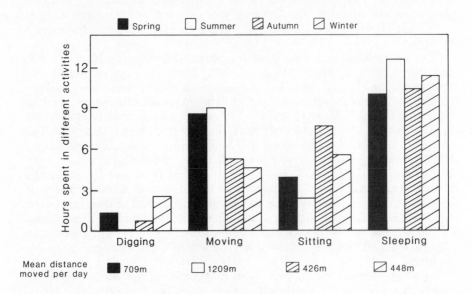

underground he could not, of course, observe their behaviour in any great detail. However, by using a variety of clues he was reasonably sure that he could determine when they were asleep, when they were sitting still in their tunnels, when they were actively moving about, and when they were digging. From these observations, Haeck was able to calculate the approximate proportion of each 24 hours that was devoted to each of these activities at different times of the year (Figure 5.2).

The results show, perhaps surprisingly, that a Dutch mole spends almost half its life fast asleep in the comfort of its nest. Our own figures from the north of Scotland are in total agreement, with both male and female moles devoting at least nine hours a day to sleep at most times of the year (Figure 5.3). However, the picture is not quite as simple as it might appear at first sight, and a closer inspection of the Scottish data will reveal that there are seasonal and sexual differences in the precise amounts of time spent in and out of the nest. For much of the year males spend a greater proportion of each day in activity than females, presumably because being heavier they have greater energy requirements and thus need to spend longer foraging for food. However, differences in size cannot be the only factor involved since the difference in the behaviour between the two sexes becomes much more marked with the onset of the breeding season in late February. At this time males go off in a frantic search for receptive females and spend increasingly less and less time in their nests. This reaches a climax in March, when males return to their nests only rarely, or not at all, instead snatching whatever sleep they can out in the cold and the wet of the tunnel systems. Only after all the females are impregnated do the males return, presumably exhausted, to their normal routine.

Figure 5.3 Seasonal changes in the proportion of the day spent in activity by European moles

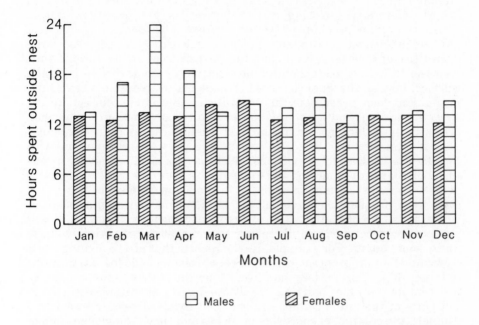

In May and June it is the turn of the females to increase their levels of activity, and for this short period of time, they actually spend a greater proportion of the day out of their nests than males. This is the time of year when they are in full lactation and consequently their energy demands are considerable, demands which can only be met by an increase in the amount of time spent searching for food.

Having slept their fill, moles spend what is left of the day out of their nests and involved in one form of activity or another. A striking and perhaps unexpected feature, given that we are dealing with a fossorial animal, is just how little time is devoted by some moles to digging. In Holland, for example, Haeck found that although most digging was carried out in the winter months, even then less than 2.5 hours per day were devoted to this activity. The onset of spring saw a progressive reduction in the amount of excavation carried out, and by the time summer came along digging occupied only a few minutes per day. Such seasonal changes in the efforts that moles put into digging are probably due largely to changes in soil conditions. During much of the autumn and winter the soil is damp and easily worked, and this is also the time when tunnels are most likely to be damaged by flooding, frost and cultivation. Consequently most tunnel excavation and repair takes place at these times of the year. However, tunnel excavation continues well into the spring, with the result that by the time summer arrives, with its hard, dry and unworkable soils, the resident mole is usually in possession of an extensive system of tunnels, and all in a good state of repair.

The amount of digging that any mole has to do during its life will, however, vary from one area to another, depending largely upon the soil conditions in which it finds itself. This has been clearly shown by Mellanby (1971) who has studied moles in a variety of habitats, each with a very different type of soil and providing very diverse quantities of food. The extremes are probably presented by areas of deciduous woodland and fenland in the south of England. The soils under forest support both large quantities of invertebrate life and high densities of moles. Despite this, however, it is rare to see signs of mole activity, such as molehills, at the surface. Instead the whole area seems to be permeated with a branching network of deep, permanent tunnels, which remain in use for generation after generation, and which seldom seem to demand repair or extension. The soils of the fenlands are in stark contrast. These areas are frequently flooded and the soil fauna is extremely sparse in comparison with woodlands. Under such conditions molehills appear almost every day as the moles labour to find food and to repair their tunnels, which must be in a state of almost permanent collapse in the sloppy, wet soils.

However frequent or infrequent an activity it may be, digging requires the expenditure of a great deal of energy, as shown in Chapter 2. It will come as no great surprise, therefore, to find that moles normally dig in quite short bursts. For example, Haeck reports that of 116 digging bouts involving four different moles, 53 per cent of them lasted for less than one minute, 73 per cent for less than five, 84 per cent for less than ten and 95 per cent for less than half an hour. These digging operations occurred in all parts of the animals' home ranges and involved repairs to existing tunnels, the creation of short side branches and the digging of new major tunnels. During all of these observations only one individual was seen to engage in long and protracted digging; on one occasion it dug continuously for 2.5 hours and on another for 4.5 hours. It seems likely, therefore, that digging in short bursts is the norm and that prolonged digging takes place only when males are seeking out females in the spring, or when a mole moves into a new area, either to create a home range for the first time or to extend an existing one. Under these circumstances moles are capable of quite tremendous efforts; Godfrey (1955) describes, for example, how one mole, establishing a territory for itself in a grass meadow, dug 20 m of deep tunnel on the first day of occupation, 3.5 m on the second day, and 24 m over the next four days.

The amount of time devoted to moving around the tunnel system, and thus the total distance covered each day, varies from one individual to another and from one season to another. In general, moles move around most in the spring and summer and least in the autumn and winter. In Holland, for instance, the distances traversed by an individual mole during the course of a single day ranged from 262 m to 1,572 m, while average distances calculated from all the different animals varied from 426 m in the autumn up to 1,209 m in the summer (Figure 5.2). Such seasonal differences are due to a combination of factors, including the fact that males are actively seeking out females in spring. In addition, both sexes, but particularly the energetically stressed lactating females, must find it harder to obtain their daily food requirements in the summer months when the soil is dry and prey animals are less mobile and lying deep in the soil. At such times moles are forced to travel further each day if they are to meet their nutritional needs.

CYCLES OF ACTIVITY

The belief has long been widespread particularly among country dwellers, that the mole digs, or 'works', at 8 o'clock, midday and 4 o'clock. (Godfrey & Crowcroft, 1960).

So far in this chapter, patterns of activity have been looked at in a rather crude way, by simply considering the proportion of an average day that is spent in rest or in one or other forms of activity. What we now want to do is to address the somewhat different question of just when, within each 24 hour period, these activities occur. As will become apparent, the country-dwellers referred to in the above quotation were almost correct in their beliefs; almost, but not quite!

Few animals are continuously active throughout the 24 hours of each day. Instead, they show more or less distinct rhythms of behaviour in which periods of activity alternate with periods of rest or sleep. The detailed structure of these rhythms varies considerably from one species to another, but in general, animals are either diurnal or nocturnal, respectively restricting their activity to daylight or to the hours of darkness. More rarely, a species may be crepuscular, with individuals concentrating their activities at the interface between light and dark at dawn and dusk. Such differences in the timing of activity are clearly adaptive and function to maximise the inclusive fitness of the species in question. Throughout their lives animals face a number of particularly challenging problems; how to get enough to eat, how to avoid being eaten, and how to minimise competition with other species having similar ecological requirements. The different patterns of activity that we see in the natural world have evolved in response to such problems and pressures. Night and day differ quite dramatically in terms of the dangers and opportunities for foraging that they present, and consequently activity is commonly concentrated in one or the other. Every species treads an evolutionary tightrope, constantly striving to strike a balance between the need to minimise the chances of falling prey to some predator and yet to forage at those times when food can be most economically gathered. In addition, ecologically similar species strive to avoid competition by dividing time up amongst themselves, in just the same way that they divide up space, food types and other vital resources.

In a sense, moles live rather charmed lives since they are largely divorced from the sorts of problems outlined above. Snug underground, in a world of constant darkness, and largely buffered from the extremes of temperature endured by surface-dwelling creatures, the regular alternation of night and day plays little part in their daily existence. For most of their lives they are relatively well protected from predators and it is an unlucky mole indeed that just happens to be foraging on the surface, or digging a superficial tunnel, when a marauding fox or buzzard chances by. Furthermore, the majority of moles face little competition from other fossorial, insectivorous mammals. Finally, these fortunate creatures can obtain food from the soil at all times of the day and night; individual prey species may undertake daily vertical migrations but the tunnels dug by moles permeate to such depths that they ensure the constant availability of food.

Against this background, one might well predict that there would be no particular advantage to a mole in being either strictly nocturnal or diurnal, and that as a result active individuals would be likely to be encountered at any time of the day or night. This certainly seems to be the case with golden moles: *Amblysomus hottentotus*, for example, shows six or seven peaks of activity spread throughout the day and night, although with some indication of increased levels of activity at dusk, midnight and dawn (Kuyper, 1985). The first indications that it might also be so with true moles came from a series of refreshingly simple experiments carried out in the USA just before the outbreak of the First World War (Scheffer, 1913). In the very best traditions of field biologists the experiments were carefully designed so that most of the work was done by the animals; Scheffer simply flattened the surface tunnels made by the moles *Scalopus* and *Parascalops* and then stood back and waited to see at what times of the day or night the damage would be made good. In the event 135 tunnels were repaired during the hours of darkness and 116 during daylight, confirming that these species, at least, are neither strictly nocturnal nor diurnal.

Some forty years later, Godfrey (1955) was able to show, with the aid of her radioactive tail rings, that European moles behave just like their distant American cousins in the sense that active individuals can be found at all times of the day and night. However, thanks to the more advanced technology at her disposal, Godfrey was able to add much more detail to the picture and to show that individual moles exhibit a regular rhythm of behaviour in which periods of rest, spent in the nest, alternate with bouts of activity out in the tunnels. In European moles, and probably in other species also, there are usually three sessions of activity and three periods of rest, each lasting for 3–4 hours, during the course of each 24 hours (Figure 5.4).

Figure 5.4 The pattern of activity of a European mole over a period of ten days. The stippled areas represent the hours of darkness

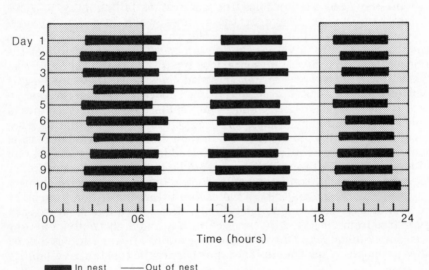

82

This is as simple a pattern of daily activity as one is likely to encounter in a mammal, and represents bouts of more or less continuous feeding, separated by periods of digestion. Among animals in general, the time that is spent foraging for a single meal will be determined partly by the availability of food but also by the capacity of the stomach. The lower and upper limits of the length of time that can elapse between meals are set, respectively, by the speed of digestion and by the rate of energy expenditure of the animal. In the case of small mammals with very high metabolic rates, for example shrews or insectivorous bats, the period for which they can safely fast, if they are not to expire, can be quite short. Shrews have solved the problem by going out to feed at very regular intervals throughout both the day and the night. Unfortunately such an option has not been open to the bats. For them to hunt during the hours of daylight would be highly dangerous because of the presence of birds of prey. In addition, they would face intense feeding competition from swallows and martins, a group of birds that had already been around for several million years when the bats first appeared. Faced with such difficulties, insectivorous bats have elected to feed only at night, and to enter a state of torpor during the day, dropping their body temperature so as to substantially reduce energy expenditure. There is some evidence that golden moles adopt this same strategy of reducing body temperature, not on a daily basis, but only during periods of food shortage. As we have already seen, *Amblysomus hottentotus* normally follows a regular routine of alternating periods of rest and activity (Figure 5.5). However, when faced with a shortage of food it responds, not by increasing its searches as one might expect, but by reducing its levels of activity and by dropping its body temperature from the normal 33.5°C down to just a couple of degrees above its surroundings. This behaviour has only rarely been observed in

Figure 5.5 The daily pattern of activity in the golden mole Amblysomus hottentotus on a restricted food supply (top) and on an ad libitum diet (bottom) (after Kuyper, 1985)

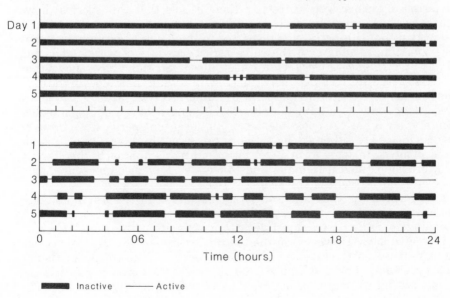

golden moles but it has recently been described in some detail by Korn (1986).

I will present some observations made on a Hottentot Golden Mole that I caught by hand after two days of heavy rain . . . I took it to the laboratory, where it was housed in a large bucket that was filled with a 15 cm thick layer of sandy soil . . . Next morning at about 7 a.m. I returned and found the mole lying on the surface. It was stretched out, stiff, cold and apparently dead. Because of urgent commitments I put the animal back to preserve it later. On my return at about 11 a.m. I was surprised to find this Golden Mole active again. Now I realised that the animal must have been in torpor during the night . . .

By about 11 p.m. the temperature in the unheated laboratory had fallen below 10°C. The Golden Mole was cold and stiff again. It could be handled like a dead body and no obvious response could be observed.

Next morning at about 9 a.m. it was already fairly warm outside and the animal was put out to the sunshine. After a while the Golden Mole started to move. At first it was very slow, but after a while it became increasingly faster. After about 30 minutes it was completely active again. Later in the day if was fed with a small amount of arthropods. In the following night the animal fell in torpor again . . . The duration of the torpor was at least 10 hours each night.

By reducing its body temperature in this way a golden mole can reduce its daily energy expenditure by at least 50 per cent. The strategy really does seem to pay dividends; Kuyper (1985) was able to show that Hottentot moles which remained active throughout a three-month period of famine lost on average over half of their body-weight, whereas individuals that regularly entered torpor lost only 5 per cent.

Returning now to the European mole, it appears that the country folk referred to earlier were correct in their beliefs that this species shows three periods of activity each day. Where they were wrong was in their assertion that this activity is restricted to the hours of daylight and that all individuals adhere to the same strict schedule of work, labouring away at 8, 12 and 4 o'clock. Our own studies in Scotland have shown that mole society runs on much more complex lines than that. Most of the data have been collected automatically by radio receivers attached to chart recorders and placed immediately above the nests of radio-tagged moles. In this way it has been possible to monitor, over long periods, the times at which moles are either asleep in their nests or out in their tunnel systems and involved in some form of activity. Using this approach, the activity patterns of 32 moles, 18 males and 14 females, have been measured over the different seasons of the year.

For most of the year the Scottish moles followed the normal, and now familiar, routine of three activity periods per day, with individuals tending to be inactive or active at approximately the same times on successive days. However, as the seasons progressed, it quickly became apparent that both sexes can on occasion deviate from this basic theme. This is clearly shown in Figure 5.6 which presents, for each month of the year, typical examples of both male and female activity rhythms. The

Figure 5.6 Seasonal changes in the activity of male and female European moles. The stippled areas represent the hours of darkness

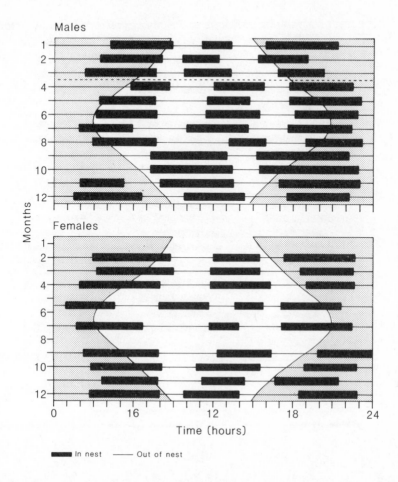

first indications of a radical change in behaviour became apparent in late March when, with the onset of breeding, the hitherto ordered lives of the males began to break down. Instead of regularly returning to their nests the males began to dig new tunnels and to travel long distances in search of mates. When fatigued by their efforts they grabbed just a few minutes' sleep in the tunnels before continuing in their quests.

In May and June it was the turn of the females to show a change in behaviour. With the birth of their young mothers tended to return to their nests four or five times per day instead of the usual three, thus allowing the growing young to be suckled more frequently.

The final change in routine occurred in September and October, when the males began to adopt a biphasic rhythm, with just two active periods per day. Despite much mental effort and head-scratching we are still unable to offer a sensible, functional explanation for this phenomenon!

We have already pointed out that individual moles tend to be active at about the same times each day. In addition, the activity cycles of

Figure 5.7 The activity patterns of five neighbouring European moles (A–E) over a four-day period. The stippled areas represent the hours of darkness

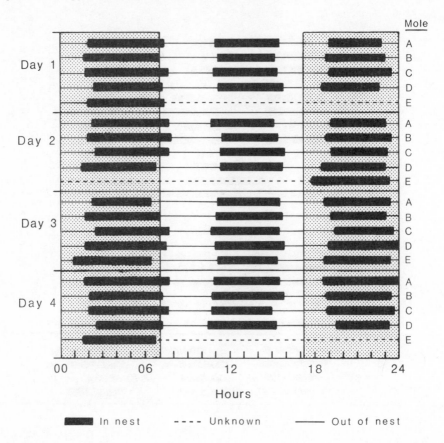

immediate neighbours are to a large extent synchronised. For an example of such behaviour take a look at Figure 5.7. This drawing depicts four days in the lives of five moles, living in adjoining home ranges in a grass field and named, rather unromantically, A, B, C, D and E. Unfortunately, the record of activity is incomplete for mole E due to instrument failure. Each of the moles showed the typical pattern of alternating rest and activity, with three active periods per day. What was most striking was the high degree of synchrony among the animals in their activity bouts, with all five leaving and returning to their nests at about the same times. This synchronisation of activity is not just of academic interest; it is an important factor in the avoidance of overt aggression between neighbours, a topic to be discussed in greater detail in the next chapter.

This vision of a temporally organised society might seem, at first sight, to be completely at odds with the results that have been presented by other workers. Both Godfrey & Crowcroft (1960) and Haeck (1969), for example, have suggested that there is little or no synchrony of activity between the different members of a population of moles. These

Figure 5.8 The relationship between the daily onset of activity in the European mole and the time of sunrise

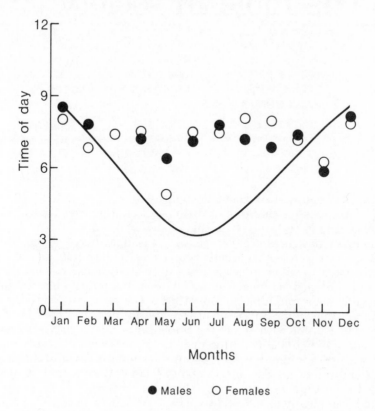

Months

● Males   ○ Females

apparently different views of mole society are probably a consequence of the fact that we have been working on rather different scales. The members of a group of immediate neighbours are highly synchronised amongst themselves, but there is much less evidence of synchrony between groups of moles which are located at some distance from each other. Consequently, if one were to monitor individuals drawn from over a relatively large area, as Godfrey & Crowcroft and Haeck did, then one would get the impression of a somewhat chaotic society, a society in which the activity of individuals was largely uncoordinated.

Finally, we might give a little thought to what factors might determine when a mole becomes active for the first time each day. In most animals sunrise is a major landmark and is frequently used to anchor the timing of the daily cycle. Although moles do come to the surface on occasion and although day-length appears to be involved in the timing of breeding (see Chapter 4), nevertheless the daily onset of activity is quite unrelated to the time of sunrise (Figure 5.8). Instead, within fairly broad limits, moles appear to commence their daily activity at about the same time each day, regardless of the time of year, or the time of sunrise. In this, as in so many other areas, there is still a very great deal to be learned about the lives of moles.

6 The mole in society

So much has been written about the aggressive nature of moles that one might be forgiven for thinking of them as the raging psychopaths of the countryside. It is certainly true that if two moles are placed together, with no immediate means of escape, they will fight fiercely, and often to the death. However, such a cruelly contrived situation tells us very little about the ways in which moles interact in the real world, beyond the fact that two frightened prisoners can inflict appalling injuries on each other. In the wild, moles might fight at any time of the year, but they do so only very rarely and, nine times out of ten, the conflict will be a brief and bloodless encounter with one of the combatants beating a hasty retreat. The majority of fights probably occur in the summer months when young, newly weaned animals are seeking out a home for themselves. If such youngsters are so unwise as to enter a tunnel system that is already occupied then they will get pretty short shrift. Such an encounter was seen and graphically described by Godfrey (1957b). The star of the piece, 'D', was a juvenile mole seeking its own territory.

> 'D' was digging just below the surface when it suddenly emerged, struggling as if held from behind. It turned and re-entered the tunnel and a fierce fight ensued, in the course of which the roof of the tunnel collapsed exposing the two moles. When they separated 'D' remained partly in view and wet bite-marks were visible on its rump. It then burrowed in the tunnel again, and another fight took place.

Apart from incidents such as these, fights are uncommon because, once established in the ground, neighbouring moles rarely meet. In order to understand how they manage to avoid one another, one needs to know something about how a mole society is organised, and how its members divide up the available space amongst themselves.

HOME RANGES AND TERRITORIES

The area in which an animal carries out its normal activities, and which provides all its needs, from food and water to the opportunity to reproduce, is called a home range. In some species the home ranges of different individuals overlap with each other to a considerable extent,

88

sometimes completely. Other species are much less tolerant of each other and individuals demand the exclusive use of an area of ground, from which they exclude conspecifics. An area which is defended in this way is called a territory. Although the defence can be vigorous on occasion, actual fighting between territorial animals is in fact quite a rare event. This is because they normally advertise the area of ground to which they lay claim, and other individuals avoid entering such occupied areas. Even when a conflict does develop between a resident animal and an intruder it is usually settled without escalation to all-out fighting. Instead conventional rules are widely employed to settle disputes, a commonly used one being that the intruder shall withdraw and the resident retain ownership. Maynard Smith (1982), having in mind the relationship between the freemen of the old French burghs and the rural peasantry, has termed this the bourgeois strategy in his book on game theory; if you are a resident then escalate until the intruder retreats; if you are an intruder then display and pull back if the resident starts to escalate to real fighting.

Faced with such very disparate lifestyles one immediately begins to wonder what the advantages of being territorial might be. Animals incur very real costs in establishing and holding a territory; time and energy must be devoted to patrolling the borders and to advertising ownership, and there is always the risk of physical injury when overt conflicts develop. Clearly, if a territorial system evolves then the benefits to be gained must outweigh the costs. Probably the most common function of territoriality amongst mammalian species is to secure a resource, particularly food.

A home range or a territory may be occupied by a varying number of individuals. At the one extreme there are the so-called solitary species in which individuals spend most of their lives in splendid isolation. However, no species is truly asocial, since all have to come together, however briefly, for the purpose of procreation. In other species, varying numbers of individuals hold a range jointly, with the members of the group sharing its resources and, in the case of group territories, the costs of defence.

ARE MOLES TERRITORIAL?

Until recently it would have been a very challenging task indeed to obtain a detailed description of the way in which populations of moles are organised. In the past it was difficult enough to obtain this kind of information for species that live on the surface, and nigh on impossible with subterranean animals. However, the position has improved dramatically in the last few years thanks to the availability of the small radio transmitters described in the last chapter. With the aid of this new technology we have been able to analyse in some depth the interactions that go on between neighbouring moles.

Most of our data have been obtained from moles living in an area of pasture at Haddo Estate, on the Buchan plain in the north-east of Scotland. Friesian traps were used to catch the moles living in a single field, and each of them was fitted with a radio transmitting on its own

Figure 6.1 The spatial organisation of mole territories as revealed by radio-telemetry. The territories are depicted as the harmonic mean isopleth containing 95 per cent of the radio fixes

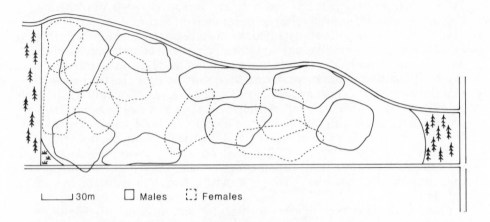

L____J 30m   □ Males   ⬚ Females

unique frequency. After some considerable effort, we were confident that we had caught all the moles living in the field, a total of 15 individuals. In order to discover the social organisation of this small population of moles, they were followed for several days, and their positions were recorded every 10–15 minutes. The result was, of course, a large number of crosses on a map showing where each animal had been found. The problem faced by all radio-trackers is how to use such radio fixes to plot and measure the area used by an individual. A variety of methods, ranging from the simple to the highly complex, have been developed over the years to achieve this. The most straightforward approach is to join up the outermost radio fixes to form a convex polygon which contains all the other fixes within its boundary. We have chosen to use a rather more complex statistical method, called the harmonic mean transformation, which depicts the range used by the animal as a set of isopleths, or contours, each containing a different proportion of the radio fixes (Dixon & Chapman, 1980). The isopleth that contained 95 per cent of the radio fixes was used as a definition of the area used by an individual as it went about its normal, daily routine.

The areas exploited by each of the 15 European moles in the study population are shown in Figure 6.1. As befits their primitive nature, moles appear to enjoy a relatively simple and straightforward social order. For most of the year established adults are solitary and sedentary creatures which occupy a mosaic of subterranean home ranges, rather like a pack of cards scattered on the ground. The areas occupied by different individuals are largely exclusive and used by only one animal, although there is a small, varying degree of overlap between the ranges of some neighbours. Typically, the ranges of neighbouring male moles do not overlap at all, but each male's range may overlap those of a variable number of females, and females may overlap with other females. By excavating areas of ground used by two individuals it became clear that the apparent overlap between adjacent ranges involves mainly the

Figure 6.2 An area of overlap between two mole territories. The tunnels of one mole are shown stippled and those of the other are shown clear. The tunnels of the two animals are connected at two points and there is much interdigitation of the tunnels within the soil column

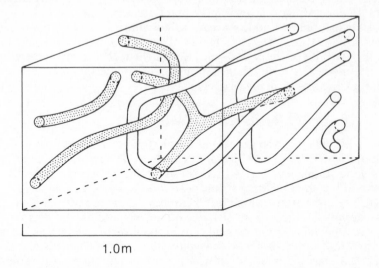

1.0m

interdigitation of tunnels in the soil column although there is also some sharing of tunnels (Figure 6.2). This explains the common observation that, whereas most mole traps will only catch one animal, some will catch several in quick succession.

The only deviation from this simple state of affairs comes in the spring when males start to seek out mates. To do so, they dig long, straight tunnels radially outwards from their own home ranges in the hope of breaking into the tunnel systems of receptive females. Such social contact is brief indeed and once the females are mated, the males retire to the solitude of their own ranges. On balance, therefore, European moles can be regarded as being solitary, territorial animals. The same is probably true of all the other species.

HOW BIG ARE MOLE TERRITORIES?

Mole territories can vary considerably in size; a female living in a lush lowland meadow may require only 300 m² of space, whereas a male eking out its life on a barren, windswept Highland muir may be defending more than 3,000 m². Why should this be so? What factors determine the size of a particular territory?

To begin at a somewhat theoretical level, it would seem intuitively likely that an individual will defend only the minimum area that is necessary to provide the key resources it requires. To defend a larger area than is strictly necessary would clearly involve increased costs and would seem, therefore, to constitute bad economics. However, there is another view, and Verner (1977) has argued that an apparently spiteful act such as defending more resources than one strictly requires, may make evolutionary sense in that doing so denies them to others and thereby reduces their relative reproductive success. Evolutionary advance can be a very dirty business indeed!

What actually constitutes a key resource will vary from individual to individual, depending, for example, upon its age and sex. However, amongst all established adults access to adequate food supplies is vital and it is likely, therefore, that levels of energy expenditure and food availability will be primary determinants of the size of a given territory. If this is indeed the case, then a number of predictions can be made concerning the sizes of mole territories.

Habitat Differences

To begin with, one would predict that for any given species of mole, those individuals which live in habitats with relatively low densities of food would defend larger territories than those fortunate enough to be living in areas with richer pickings. European moles, for example, live in a broad variety of habitats which differ greatly in the amount of food that they can supply, ranging from rich deciduous woodlands and permanent pastures at the one extreme to acid coniferous forests and barren coastal sand-dunes at the other. Over the years there have been attempts to measure the sizes of mole territories in a number of these habitats. Unfortunately, different techniques have been used in the different studies, but on the whole they have been sufficiently similar to allow valid comparisons to be made. The results totally support the prediction, with an inverse relationship between territory size and the density of food in the ground (Figure 6.3). Thus, in Britain, moles living in deciduous woodlands and lowland pastures, where food densities are around 200–250 g of invertebrates per square metre, occupy small ranges of between 300 and 400 m². In contrast, we have found that moles living on a coastal sand-dune system in Aberdeenshire, and enjoying a pitiful

Figure 6.3 The relationship between food density (vertical bars) and territory size in European moles. For ease of comparison the territories are shown as circles

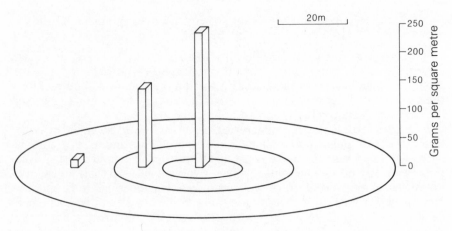

food supply of only 2.0–2.5 g m^{-2}, take for themselves territories in excess of 5,000 m^2.

The Effects of Body Size

One would also predict that male moles, being bigger than females and thus burdened with greater rates of energy expenditure, should occupy correspondingly larger territories. We have a body of data, collected in the north-east of Scotland, which suggests that this is indeed so. In order to avoid the inevitable complications that arise as a result of reproduction, and which will be dealt with shortly, we will for the moment restrict ourselves to a consideration of the sizes of territories outside the breeding season. Measurements were made of a number of non-breeding territories in two quite distinct habitats, a coastal pasture and a plantation of mixed deciduous trees dominated by beech. Both the habitats lay on top of a thin sandy soil, and each had a relatively low density of food. In each the male moles occupied territories which were larger than those of the females, on average 1.6 times as large in the pasture and 1.7 times in the woodland (Table 6.1). These differences are to a large extent explicable in terms of rates of energy expenditure. As explained in Chapter 2, basal metabolic rates (R_s) are a function of body-weight (W), and are described by the following formula:

$$R_b = 4.1W^{0.751}$$

where the units are watts and kilograms.

Using this formula, the metabolic rate of an average-sized Scots male mole (107 g) works out at about 0.76 watts and that of an average 75 g female at 0.59 watts, a ratio of 1.3:1.0. Thus the ratios between the range sizes (1.6:1.0) and between the metabolic rates (1.3:1.0) of the two sexes are clearly similar. They are not identical, but one would hardly expect them to be, given the relatively small sample sizes, the inaccuracies involved in measuring territory size, and the fact that the energy expenditure calculations are based on average-sized animals whereas the estimates of territory size clearly are not.

Differences Due to Breeding

A striking feature of the annual cycle, and one that has been alluded to several times already, is the way in which male moles expand their ranges at the beginning of the breeding season, as they begin to sniff out

Table 6.1 Seasonal differences in the sizes of mole territories in north-east Scotland

Mean Territory Size (square metres)

Habitat	Breeding Male	Non-breeding Male	Breeding Female	Non-breeding Female
Pasture	7343	2679	1314	1655
Woodland	7718	3364	2086	1945

receptive females. In both of the Scottish habitats the males more than doubled the sizes of their territories during the mating season (Table 6.1), and thereby greatly increased their chances of encountering breeding partners. However, the expansion was a transitory phenomenon and once the rut was over the males returned to the areas that they had previously occupied.

Surprisingly, the females living in these study areas did not expand their territories during the breeding season. We say surprisingly, because females incur substantially increased energy demands during breeding, particularly during lactation. Other species of insectivores, for example the shrews *Sorex vagrans* and *Sorex obscurus*, behave more as one might expect and double the sizes of their territories when they have dependent young to support (Hawes, 1975). The fact that moles do not adopt this strategy can be explained in two ways, neither explanation being mutually exclusive. On the one hand it could be that females hold larger ranges in the autumn and winter than they actually need at those times in anticipation of their increased demands during breeding. Equally, it may be the case that the amount of food available in the territory increases sufficiently during the spring to satisfy the females' increased requirements.

Clearly, therefore, there is no simple answer to the question of how big a mole territory is. It depends on the mole in question, where it lives, what sex it is, and of course, the season of the year.

COMMUNICATION BETWEEN NEIGHBOURS

Despite their subterranean and lonely lifestyle, moles are very much aware of the presence and behaviour of their neighbours. There are two lines of evidence in support of this contention. The first comes from a number of experiments in which moles were removed from their territories, and the second from a detailed study of temporal patterns in the way that individual moles exploit their ranges.

Except in the breeding season, moles normally remain strictly within the confines of their own tunnel system. However, if a mole dies, or if it is removed from its range by a predator, angry gardener or inquisitive scientist, neighbouring animals will move, often rapidly, into the vacated area. Such behaviour is exemplified in Figure 6.4 which shows the ranges of two sets of four neighbouring moles living on the Haddo Estate. The upper parts of the figure show, in each case, the spatial organisation of the moles' ranges based on data gathered over several weeks. When the moles, whose ranges are shown stippled, were trapped and removed, one or more of the neighbouring animals moved into and occupied parts of the vacated areas. In both cases, the detection of the trapped animal's disappearance was rapid, with the first neighbour encroaching on the empty area within 15 hours. Clearly, moles are well aware of whether an area is currently occupied or empty.

If moles should meet outside the breeding season, serious fighting is the usual outcome. The fact that this is an infrequent event provides the basis for the second line of evidence. Despite the fact that their ranges

Figure 6.4 Two examples of the responses of European moles to the demise of a neighbour. The upper part of each figure shows the situation before the removal of one individual. The lower parts show subsequent changes in the extent of the territories of the remaining moles

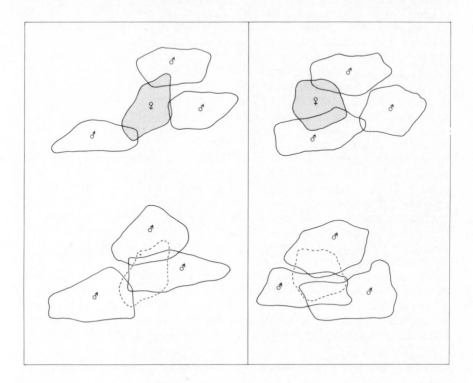

frequently overlap, neighbouring moles rarely come into direct contact with each other, and so avoid the risk of overt aggression. Instead, they show temporal avoidance with only one individual using an area held in common at any one time. This was clearly demonstrated by the group of five moles whose overlapping ranges and patterns of activity are shown in Plate 17 and Figure 5.7. These animals displayed the typical pattern of alternating rest and activity with three periods per day that we described in the previous chapter. In addition the activity of the moles was highly synchronised with all five leaving and returning to their nests at about the same time. Thoughout the period that these animals were radio-tracked, the area of overlap between the ranges of any two neighbours was exploited by only one individual during any given period of activity. This is clearly demonstrated in Plates 18–20, which also show the way in which all five moles exploited their ranges during three consecutive periods of activity. In these three-dimensional maps the vertical dimension reflects the number of times an animal was located in different parts of its range. It is clear that although these animals were sharing areas of ground, and probably also tunnels, nevertheless they did so at different times of the day, and thus avoided meeting each other.

Olfactory Communication

Clearly, moles are not only aware of the fact that an area of ground is occupied, they also have sufficient appreciation of the movement patterns of their neighbours to avoid meeting them in the areas of range overlap. This implies that information is being passed, by one means or another, between individuals. Mammals communicate with each other in a variety of ways. Sometimes signals are passed visually, sometimes by sound, and very often by social odours. As a group, the mammals are equipped with a dazzling variety of specialised odoriferous skin glands, and their profligate use of the olfactory opportunities presented by their urine and faeces can be, quite literally, breath-taking. As signals, social odours have a number of distinct advantages; for example, they can be deposited as scent marks in the environment, where they provide a spatial and historical record of an individual's movements and behaviour. Scent marks also have the important property of remaining active as signals for extended periods of time, even in the absence of their producer. It is not surprising, therefore, that scent marking is widely used by mammals as a means of advertising land tenure. The system has the added advantage that it is cheat-proof in the sense that only a long-term resident can have had the opportunity to pepper an area with its own recognisable scent marks.

For moles olfactory communication has a number of advantages over other forms of signalling. For example, it is fully effective underground, whereas visual and auditory signals are of limited or no value in that environment. Both male and female moles have a pair of scent glands known as preputial glands which lie beneath the skin and which are thus

Figure 6.5 Seasonal changes in the weights of the preputial scent glands of European moles

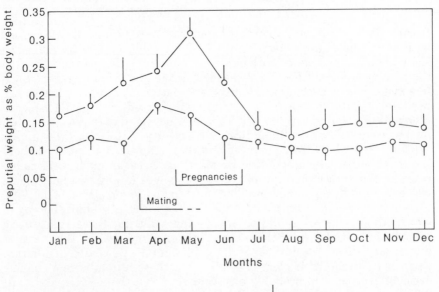

96

normally invisible (Plate 16). The glands, which contain both apocrine and sebaceous elements, open into the urethra, that part of the urinary tract that leads from the bladder to the outside world, and add to the voided urine a secretion with an odour reminiscent of the general smell of a mole. The preputial glands of males are larger than those of females, even allowing for sexual differences in body-weight, but they increase in weight in both sexes during the breeding season (Figure 6.5). The secretion produced by the glands contains a complex mixture of volatile chemicals with marked individual and sexual differences in composition (Gorman & Stone, in press). There is the potential, therefore, for moles to use urine containing preputial secretions to signal that a territory is occupied or that a resident animal is currently active in a given area of tunnels. Mole ranges contain several hundreds of metres of tunnels and thus quite large quantities of urine will be required if the range is to be marked on the regular basis that seems to be needed to repel neighbours. Thanks to the nature of their diet, moles do in fact produce copious quantities of urine. As explained earlier, the average mole consumes around 60 g of earthworms each day, containing some 50 g of water. Given the high humidity of the tunnel system, most of the water taken in will be voided as urine.

Where do moles urinate? Although urine is produced in relatively large quantities it is nevertheless a finite and limited resource. One would predict, therefore, that if urine is indeed used for scent marking then moles will not urinate randomly, but in an organised pattern that maximises the chances of the urinations being encountered by other moles. In order to test this prediction and to investigate the pattern in which urine is dispersed in the territory we first determined, by radio-tracking, the extent of a male mole's range and the positions of its tunnel. The animal was then recaptured and injected with a small quantity of ^{32}P, a radioactive isotope which is slowly excreted via the urine. This accomplished, the mole was released back into its tunnel system for a further 48 hours, after which time it was caught and killed in a Duffus trap. A section of the mole's territory was then carefully excavated and all the tunnels in that area monitored for signs of radioactivity. All the places where the level of radiation was at least 100 per cent above background and where there was no evidence of faecal material are shown in Figure 6.6. It is clear that, as predicted, urine was deposited at distinct sites throughout the tunnel system; particularly noteworthy is the fact that all the tunnel junctions were marked in this way, thus maximising the chance of scent marks being discovered by an intruding animal, regardless of its direction of travel.

The abdominal fur of live moles is usually stained brown and smells strongly of preputial secretion. When we measured levels of radioactivity on the fur of the injected mole it became obvious that urine, and therefore preputial secretion, had been dispersed over much of the ventral surface. It seems likely, therefore, that in addition to direct marking with urine, odorous material will also become smeared onto the floors of the tunnels as moles move around.

How do moles react to urine and preputial secretions? If scent is used to signal that an area is occupied then one would expect moles, under some circumstances, to actively avoid the odours produced by other individuals.

Figure 6.6 *An excavated area of the tunnel system of a European mole. The circles represent places where the mole had urinated*

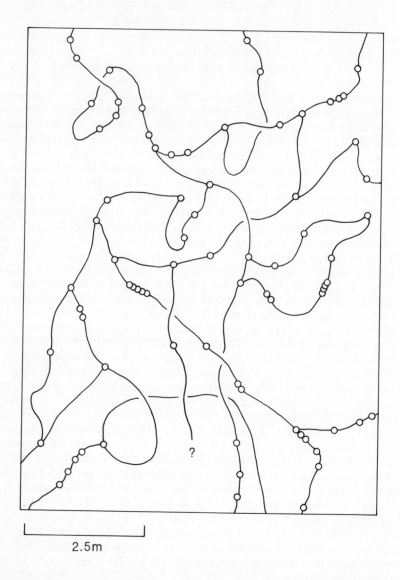

2.5m

We have, therefore, carried out behavioural trials to test this prediction in the field, using as subjects free-living, wild moles. The first approach was to compare the catching efficiency of clean Friesian traps with that of traps which had recently contained a mole. If moles do avoid mole odours then one would expect the soiled traps to be less efficient than the clean ones. All the traps used in the study were first made 'clean' by thoroughly washing them in a 10 per cent solution of a powerful laboratory detergent, and then rinsing them in water before leaving them to dry for several days. Finally they were buried in soil for several

Table 6.2 The trapping efficiency of Friesian traps

Number of captures in:	
Clean Traps	Soiled Traps
28	11

days since, in our experience, this increases the chances of successfully capturing moles. In order to produce 'soiled' traps a captive male mole was placed in a clean trap and allowed to wallow in it for 3–4 hours just prior to use. At the end of this treatment the soil trap smelled strongly of mole, even to the puny human nose.

Overall, an equal trapping effort was made with each of the two types of trap. In order to cope with any temporal variations in trapability, equal numbers of clean and soiled traps were set during any given month. Only one trap was set in any one mole territory and each was left in place for up to 72 hours, with daily resetting of traps if a mole blocked them off with soil.

The numbers of moles caught by the clean and soiled traps are shown in Table 6.2. Clearly the traps which had recently contained a mole were markedly less efficient at catching moles than clean ones. One must conclude, therefore, that outside the breeding season at least, moles detect, and avoid, the odours left by other moles.

The second approach to the problem was to place cotton buds, some clean, some smeared with preputial gland secretion, into the tunnels of radio-tagged moles and to determine their response when they came into close contact with them. Five moles, three males and two females, were used in the trials. Each was tracked until a good knowledge of their tunnel systems and usual movement patterns had been obtained. Having achieved this, particular sites which individual moles tended to visit on a regular basis were identified. For the sake of convenience, the sites chosen were usually shallow surface tunnels. It was then possible to place a stimulus into a tunnel, via a small hole in the roof, some 10–15 minutes before a mole was likely to arrive at that spot. The reaction of a mole reaching a stimulus was scored as follows: a positive response, with the mole retreating back down the tunnel in the direction from which it had come; a negative response, with the mole passing the stimulus and continuing along the tunnel; an unclear response, where we were uncertain what had happened. All the presentations were blind in the sense that the person doing the radio-tracking was unaware of the nature of the stimulus.

The secretions presented to the moles came from trapped animals whose glands had been removed shortly after death and then stored at $-25°C$. All the donor animals were strangers to the test moles with the exception of one male who had been an immediate neighbour of male number 3 (Table 6.3). A total of 73 control and 78 experimental presentations were made. Only one presentation was made to any one mole on any given day. The stimulus was then removed and the tunnel repaired as best we could. Subsequent presentations were made in different parts of the moles' ranges.

Table 6.3 The response of free-living moles to clean cotton buds and to cotton buds smeared with the secretions of preputial glands

Mole number	Type of stimulus	Positive	Response: Negative	Unclear
Male 1	Strange male	15	2	3
	control	2	16	2
Male 2	Strange female	15	1	1
	control	0	15	1
Male 3	Familiar male	10	0	0
	control	1	10	0
Female 1	Strange female	11	2	3
	control	0	16	0
Female 2	Strange male	10	1	4
	control	1	7	2

The reactions of the radio-tagged moles to the stimuli placed in their tunnels are shown in Table 6.3. The responses were marked and clearcut, with moles almost always retreating when they encountered preputial secretions, regardless of the sex of the donor or whether it was a stranger or familiar neighbour. As predicted, moles do avoid preputial secretions, thus lending strong support to the idea that these chemicals are involved in signalling occupancy. In order to gain further insight into whether preputial glands are involved in the day-to-day maintenance of territorial integrity we carried out a field experiment involving the removal of a resident animal, and the subsequent marking of some of its tunnels with its preputial secretions. The trial involved a triad of moles (two males and one female), and was carried out in October. Initially, the ranges of the three neighbours were determined, by radio-tracking, over a period of around ten days. Those tunnels in the areas of range overlap which were used by two individuals were identified and marked with pegs. One of the animals was then caught in a Duffus trap and its preputial glands were removed. A number of cotton buds were then smeared in the secretion and distributed in the tunnels used by the deceased mole and by one of its neighbours. An equal number of clean cotton buds were spread in the tunnels in the area of overlap with the second neighbour. The subsequent movements of the remaining animals were then followed for several days. The results of the experiment are shown in the two parts of Figure 6.7. The upper part of the figure shows the ranges occupied by the three animals prior to the removal of female 28 at 7 a.m. on 10 October. Following her demise, cotton buds smeared with her preputial secretions were placed in those tunnels that she had exploited jointly with male 41. The ranges used by the two males in the week following the removal of the female are shown in the lower part of the figure. At 3 a.m. on 11 October male 40 entered, for the first time, the now unoccupied range and remained there for the next 2.5 hours, before retiring to his own nest. At the beginning of the next activity period (the scented and unscented cotton buds having been renewed) male 40 again entered the deceased

Figure 6.7 An experiment in territorial advertisement and defence. The percentage values refer to the degree of overlap between adjacent ranges. See text for details

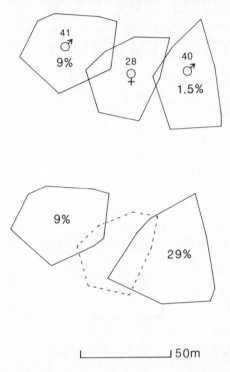

female's range and remained there for the whole of that activity period. Male 40 continued to use parts of the female's range until at least 21 October when the radios failed. Throughout this period there was no indication that male 41 entered the empty range.

7 Getting rid of a surfeit of moles

The burrowing habits of moles, and the consequent raising of molehills and surface runs, inevitably brings these otherwise innocuous creatures into direct conflict with those humans who strive to make their own mark upon the land. Sometimes the damage moles cause amounts only to a minor nuisance, causing a varying degree of consternation, indignation and raised blood pressure among amateur gardeners, but causing no real monetary loss. In other circumstances, particularly in agricultural land, the damage can take on a rather more serious complexion, with heavy infestations giving rise to distinct financial problems.

Newly cultivated and planted arable fields are a particular delight to moles, since they can move through the friable surface soil with great ease to partake of a readily garnered meal. In doing so they may disturb the roots of the young plants to such an extent that they wilt or die. The sight of a long drill of dead plants is likely to provoke retaliatory measures in even the most sanguine of farmers, even though the damage often looks much worse than it really is. Later on in the year, large molehills may cause damage to the blades of mowing machines and grain harvesters, and cause expensive delays in the progress of the harvest.

In pastureland, heavy infestations of moles may throw up so much soil that an appreciable proportion of the grazing area is lost. The subsequent reduction in the density of the stock that can be supported on the land is particularly serious in marginal upland areas. Unfortunately, it is in just such areas that the soils tend to be the poorest, with the result that the moles are forced to do a lot of digging as they seek out the meagre prey.

In Great Britain, the most important type of damage is the contamination by molehills of the grass used to make silage. The soil is a major cause of poor fermentation and preservation of the silage which is thus rendered relatively unpalatable and lacks nutritional value. To make matters worse, silage that has been badly contaminated with soil can cause severe scouring in cattle and other stock.

It is difficult to put a precise figure on the financial losses that are caused by moles. The Ministry of Agriculture, Food and Fisheries estimates that the annual cost to British agriculture in the late 1980s was of the order of £2.5 million. This sum, which includes not only the

Figure 7.1 A variety of mole traps: scissor trap (top left); Duffus half-barrel (top right); a pit-fall with trapdoor from Wales (bottom left); American harpoon trap (bottom right)

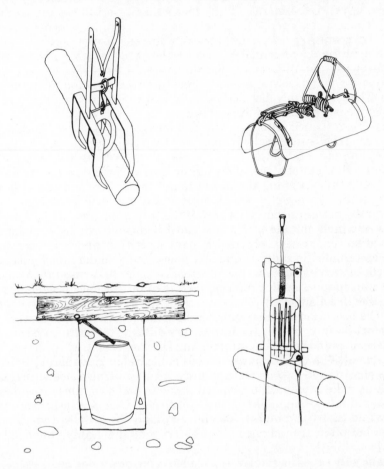

financial loss but also the cost of control measures, might seem to be a trifling sum in an industry with an annual turnover measured in billions of pounds per annum. However, national figures such as these ignore the patchy nature of the problem. Moles can have a serious impact at a local level, particularly in marginal areas where farmers may already be struggling to survive. What might be a minor irritation to a lowland grain baron may spell financial ruin for a beleaguered hill farmer.

TRAPPING

For those faced with a mole problem there are two main ways in which the animals can be destroyed, by trapping or by poisoning. Both can be pretty barbaric methods at times. In days gone by, a wide variety of traps and snares were manufactured by rural blacksmiths and carpenters (Figure 7.1). Today, however, only two main types of trap remain in wide usage, the scissor trap and the Duffus, or half-barrel, trap. Neither model is baited; they depend upon the unsuspecting mole blundering into a trigger which releases the killing mechanism. Both types are equipped with strong springs and kill by crushing. In the United Kingdom, Section 8 of the Pests Act (1954) largely prohibits the use of spring traps for catching animals, presumably because they are thought to be too cruel. However, the Small Ground Vermin Traps Order (1958) exempts from the ban spring traps that are commonly used for catching moles in their runs. The logic of this distinction is difficult to understand; perhaps it is simply a case of 'out of sight, out of mind'?

The scissor trap is equipped with two spring-loaded pairs of jaws which, when the trap is set, are held apart by means of a trigger consisting of a loose plate of metal (Figure 7.1). If the plate is disturbed by a mole it instantly flips out of place, allowing the jaws to come together with great force, and thus catching the mole around the thorax and crushing it to death. If the trap is well set, and in good condition, death is usually rapid, but rarely instantaneous. However, if the trap is old and rusty it may not crush the mole but simply hold it until it dies of exhaustion, shock or starvation. The scissor trap, which many mole-trappers prefer, is best set in deep tunnels. In order to do so, it is necessary to dig a hole just large enough to accommodate it, taking great care not to damage the run or to allow soil to fall into it. The trap must then be carefully bedded into the tunnel with soil and turfs, so as to exclude the light, but taking every care that the operation of the trap is not impeded.

Unfortunately, the scissor trap is very difficult to set in loose soil or in surface runs and in such situations the Duffus is the trap of choice. This trap consists of a half-barrel of metal from which hang two spring-activated loops of wire and two triggers (Figure 7.1). The trap is thus capable of catching moles approaching from either end, and sometimes it will catch two at a single setting. When a mole touches the trigger the loop of wire is drawn up tightly around it, hopefully around the body so that death is rapid, but often around one of its legs, with an inevitably prolonged and bloody end.

Finally there is the relatively rare harpoon, or guillotine, trap (Figure 7.1). This consists of a framework of flat metal bars which are pronged at the bottom so that they can be thrust into the soil. Across the top of the framework there is a bar through which passes a vertical metal rod, the lower end of which is welded to a plate bearing long and sharp steel spikes. The part of the rod which lies above the horizontal bar is encased in a strong coiled spring. To set the trap the spiked plate is pushed upwards, thus compressing the spring, until it engages against a notch in a hinged catch which acts as a trigger. The major advantage of the harpoon trap is that it requires no excavation of the tunnel and is thus easy to set. Having located a suitable shallow tunnel, the trapper merely presses down a section with his foot and then places the armed trap over the depression with the trigger plate flush on the soil surface. When the mole comes across the depression in the tunnel roof it may try to raise it with its powerful head and shoulders. The trigger plate is activated and releases the spring, thus driving the wicked spikes down into the ground, and through the mole. If the mole is lucky it will be speared through a vital organ, otherwise it will face a slow and agonising death. This deadly device was extremely popular in the days before the fashion for moleskin breeks and waistcoats put a premium on unblemished pelts. In Britain today, harpoon traps are to be found only in museums and country antique shops but they are still manufactured and put to practical use in the United States.

To set mole traps successfully is a highly skilled and very time-consuming job. Given the ever rising costs of labour, it is hardly surprising to find that fewer and fewer moles are trapped each year. Indeed, as a serious means of control, trapping is now largely restricted to situations where time and cost are of little consequence, as for example in the case of the amateur gardener. A thirst for revenge might also have a part to play in the matter. 'For the gardener who wants rid of a mole which is spoiling the appearance of his lawn, there is no doubt that mole trapping is a most satisfying pursuit.' (Godfrey & Crowcroft, 1960).

POISONING

In the fiercely commercial world of agriculture the more usual method of eradication is poisoning. The substance that is most commonly used for this purpose is strychnine, a highly toxic alkaloid derived from the Asiatic tree *Strychnos nux-vomica*. Raw strychnine varies somewhat in purity and toxicity and for that reason it is normally used as one of its salts, usually the sulphate or hydrochloride. In Great Britain the sale or supply of strychnine to the public is prohibited under the Pharmacy and Poisons Act, 1933. However, an exception is made for people who require it for the express purpose of killing moles and who have written authority from the Ministry of Agriculture, Food and Fisheries (MAFF), or, in Scotland, from the Department of Agriculture and Fisheries for Scotland (DAFS). Such authorities are only issued to people conversant with the use of the poison, and with its inherent dangers, and each authority is normally restricted to no more than six grams.

The major advantages of poisoning over trapping are that it requires little skill on the part of the poisoner, and once the poison is laid no further action is required, with a consequent saving of time and effort. The usual method of deploying the poison is to use large earthworms, preferably *Lumbricus terrestris*, as a poison bait. MAFF recommend that the red-brown earthworm known as the brandling (*Eisenia foetida*), which is common in manure and compost heaps, should not be used as it is thought to be unpalatable to moles. The worms are normally treated by mixing them with the strychnine in a suitable receptacle, such as a clearly and permanently labelled tin can; two grams will treat at least 100 large worms and, theoretically at least, they will kill an equal number of moles. The earthworms and strychnine must be well stirred together with a stick so that each worm becomes coated with poison. The mixture is then left to stand for 20 minutes or so before bait-laying commences. It is very important that the baits be used while they are still fresh and certainly within six hours. Thereafter they begin to decompose and become unacceptable to the mole, which is a very fastidious eater. Many experienced mole poisoners adopt a more subtle approach and prefer to soak a cotton thread in a solution of strychnine and then to thread it through the centre of a worm with the aid of a darning needle. This may well be an advantage since strychnine is very bitter to the taste and when applied to the outside of a worm it may render it less palatable and so reduce the chances of the bait being taken.

The treated worms are then laid, singly, in tunnels at points scattered throughout the infested area. When a suitable tunnel is located a hole is made with a stick or dibber, and the bait carefully inserted by means of a thin pointed stick or a long pair of forceps. The hole is then carefully sealed to prevent the ingress of light, which acts as the clearest possible warning to the mole that all is not well. In the hands of a skilled operator, 25 poisoned worms will suffice to clear the moles from a hectare of land, although several baitings may be necessary to ensure the complete eradication of a heavy infestation.

Strychnine is highly toxic, not only to moles but also to other forms of wildlife and to domestic animals. It is important, therefore, that the poisoned worms be placed in deep tunnels rather in surface runs, where they are likely to be dug up by other mammals or birds, or exposed by subsequent harrowing of the ground. Strychnine also kills humans and those with a concern for their lives, and the lives of their families, would be well advised to avoid using as receptacles for the poison any containers such as jam jars that might find their way back into the kitchen! A small quantity of strychnine goes a terrifyingly long way, and as little as 5 mg is quite capable of killing an adult man.

The major problem with using strychnine as a poison is that it kills in the most appallingly cruel manner. It is astonishing that its use continues to be condoned in the United Kingdom, a country whose citizens pride themselves on their great concern for animal welfare. Perhaps the reason for this apparent lack of concern is that few people actually witness the death agonies of poisoned moles. Were they to die in the full glare of public view, rather than in the depths of the countryside, and then often underground, there can be little doubt that there would be an outcry of such magnitude that the use of this awful material would be quickly proscribed.

To get a feel for the very real torture that is inflicted on many thousands of moles each year one might turn to the medical literature where the symptoms of strychnine poisoning in humans are described. The more modern texts tend to use highly technical terms which give little indication, to the lay mind, of the severity of the suffering that is involved. For example:

> This potent alkaloid acts in the body primarily as a central nervous stimulant. There is greatly increased reflex excitability in the spinal cord which results in a loss of the normal inhibition of spread of motor cell stimulation . . . (Arena, 1974).

For a more graphic description, and one with which we can all empathise, it is necessary to delve into the dusty treatises written in Victorian times. The following extract, taken from a book entitled *Principles of Forensic Medicine* and written by Professor W. A. Guy in 1868, should suffice.

> At an interval of from a few minutes to an hour or more after swallowing . . . the symptoms of poisoning set in with a feeling of suffocation and difficulty of breathing, the patient complaining of

want of air. These feelings of distress are soon followed by twitchings of the muscles, and jerking movements of the head and limbs, which shortly become heightened into tetanic convulsions. The arms are flexed and tightly drawn across the chest, the legs forcibly extended and widely separated, and the feet often turned inwards or outwards, the head bent back, and the whole body arched so as to rest on the head and heels. The muscles of the abdomen are rigidly contracted, respiration is suspended, the pulse is very rapid, the face is livid and congested, the eyes prominent and staring, and the features drawn into a grin. The patient complains of a choking sensation, and of thirst and dryness of the throat; but the effort to drink often occasions rigid spasms of the muscles of the jaw. Sometimes there is foaming at the mouth, and the froth is occasionally tinged with blood. The violent contractions of the muscles are accompanied by pain at the pit of the stomach and cramps in the limbs, and by intense suffering and distress. After the spasms have lasted for one or two minutes there is a remission of short duration, and the patient remains exhausted, and bathed in sweat. The fits sometimes return without apparent cause, but they may be brought on by the slightest touch, or the least effort. The mind is unaffected till towards the final termination, and may even continue clear to the last. The patient is generally quite conscious of his danger, and aware of the approach of his fits, which he announces by screams or shrieks, or by calling out that 'they are coming'; . . . In poisoning by strychnine, as in tetanus, there are violent paroxysms of rigid convulsion, with intense suffering; and in both the mind is little if at all affected; and when it does suffer, it is apparently as the result of the exquisite tortures which the patient has undergone. Towards the fatal termination, the fits become more frequent and severe, and the patient dies exhausted, or suffocated, in most cases within two hours of the commencement of the symptoms.

There is no reason at all to believe that the sufferings of the poisoned mole are in any way less awful.

OTHER METHODS OF ERADICATION

Despite the havoc that moles manage to wreak, at least on a local level, most people still feel a begrudging affection for the creatures, often so much so that they are unwilling to get involved in the cruelty that is inevitably associated with trapping or poisoning. As a result, liberally minded country folk have put much thought and ingenuity into devising means of repelling moles, that is to say, of making their lives so uncomfortable that they move away, to become someone else's problem.

The methods that are used usually involve crude assaults on one or other of the moles' sensory systems. A well-known, but probably quite useless, attempt at repulsion is to introduce prickly vegetation, such as brambles or rose prunings, into the tunnel system. The thinking behind this approach seems to be that the mole, shambling along its tunnel, will impale its super-sensitive snout on one of the barbs, and will thus be rendered so distraught that it will pack up and leave. Some chance! Any mole worth its salt will detect the interference with its tunnel long before it runs into the ambush and will simply dig its way around it. We can guarantee that the gardener will lose interest in pruning roses and opening up tunnels long before the mole will tire of digging.

Another, quite different, remedy that is often advocated involves an assault upon the ears rather than on the nose. This form of retaliation involves burying empty lemonade or beer bottles up to their necks in the ground. The wind, blowing across the open mouths of the bottles, is said to set up low-frequency vibrations which permeate through the soil and so upset the moles. A variation on the same theme involves placing a milk bottle, neck down, in the tunnel, and suspending above it a metal ring with several nails attached. When the wind blows, the nails tinkle merrily on the glass and the sound is transmitted through the tunnels, to the intense annoyance of the mole. At least that is the theory. There is, in fact, every chance that the unhappy gardener will end up worse off then ever: not only will the garden continue to be littered with molehills, it will also look quite ridiculous with its crop of emergent beer or milk bottles. For those with a surfeit of money, or a lack of bottles, there are now available high-tech versions of this ancient method, such as the battery-powered Kestrel Mole-Mover. This ingenious device consists of a control box and a long probe which is pushed into the mole-infested ground, and which periodically transmits low-frequency pressure waves through the ground, in the manner of a miniature road drill.

Moles might well be able to put up with briars in their tunnels, they might even enjoy a continual cacophony of howling beer bottles or throbbing electronic devices, but can they tolerate foul odours? Many people cherish the idea that they surely cannot, and a popular solution to a mole problem is to try and stink them out. Some of the truly imaginative substances that have been used for this purpose are described by Armsby (1952) who writes 'To drive moles away, without destroying them, all that is needed is to make the run distasteful. Their delicate sense of smell can be offended by inserting moth balls, carbide, bad fish, tar or creosote into the tunnel.'

Whether these particular substances really do repel moles we do not know, but there is evidence that they will indeed avoid some classes of aromatic substances. With a view to developing new and less cruel methods of mole control we have investigated the responses of wild, free-living moles to a number of naturally occurring odorous chemicals. We have already described, in Chapter 6, how moles are repelled by the preputial gland secretions of their own kind. In addition we have also looked at their responses to the malodorous social scents that are produced by mustelid carnivores. This might seem to be a pretty bizarre thing to do, but the reader can be assured that there is method behind this apparent experimental madness!

Carnivores frequently mark their ranges or territories with odorous faeces, urine and the secretions of skin glands. These substances also inevitably impart a powerful odour to the animals themselves. It can be safely assumed that such scent-marking behaviour confers some benefit to the carnivore in its social relationships and interactions with other members of the same species. However, there is a price to be paid for gaining such advantage, in that a predator's rank odour may give an early warning of its presence in the area to potential prey, thus allowing them to take appropriate evasive action. There is plenty of evidence to suggest that prey take full advantage of this design flaw in the behaviour of carnivores. For example, if field voles, *Microtus agrestis*, are confronted with the odours of their major predators, the stoat, *Mustela erminea*, the weasel, *Mustela nivalis*, or the red fox, *Vulpes vulpes*, they will actively avoid them, thereby reducing their chances of bumping into the predator itself, and increasing their chances of survival (Gorman, 1984; Stoddart, 1976). Avoidance responses of this kind have been used in various attempts at biological control of the feeding damage that is done by mammalian herbivores to vulnerable vegetation, for example to young saplings. Thus 3-propyl-1,2-dithiolane and 2,2-dimethylthietane, a pair of outstandingly disgusting chemical compounds from the anal sacs of stoats and mink, *Mustela vison*, have been shown to inhibit the feeding of snowshoe hares, *Lepus americanus* (Sullivan & Crump, 1984). In the same vein, piles of the foetid faeces of wolverines, *Gulo gulo*, lynx, *Felis lynx*, and bobcat, *Felis rufus*, are all effective in reducing damage by snowshoe hares and by black-tailed deer, *Odocoileus hemionus*.

Encouraged by success stories such as these, we have studied the responses of moles to the secretions produced by the anal sacs of weasels and to a synthetic version of a major component of mink scent, a foul sulphur-containing molecule known chemically as 2,2-dimethylthietane. The reader might well be surprised at this choice of materials, given that neither the weasel nor the mink are major predators of the mole. However, the aversive reactions of prey seem to be elicited by the odours of predators in general and not just by those with which the prey might be familiar. Some dramatic evidence for this is provided by the Orkney vole, *Microtus arvalis orcadensis*, which is repelled by the scent of stoats, despite the fact that the vole has been completely isolated from both stoats and weasels for over 5,000 years, ever since it was introduced to the Orkney Islands by Neolithic settlers from continental Europe (Gorman, 1984). Further, and equally compelling, evidence for the innate and general nature of these behavioural responses, comes from the fact that English field voles, *Microtus agrestis*, avoid the urine of tigers, *Panthera tigris*, and red deer, *Cervus elaphus*, avoid the dung of African lions, *Panthera leo*!

An initial approach to determining whether moles do avoid these predator scents involved comparing the catching efficiency of clean Friesian traps with that of traps tainted with weasel odour, with 2,2-dimethylthietane or with oil of peppermint. If moles are repelled by predator odours then applying them to traps should render them relatively ineffective. The peppermint treatment was included to control for the possibility that moles might respond to an odour because it is novel rather than because it signals predator.

The trapping was carried out over the winter, from November to January, with an equal trapping effort for each of the four trap types. Only one trap was set in any one mole territory, and each was left in place for up to four days with daily resetting if a mole was so unsporting as to

Table 7.1 **The trapping efficiency of Friesian traps tainted with different odours**

Clean Traps	Peppermint Traps	Weasel Traps	Dimethylthietane Traps
	Number of catches in:		
12	14	1	2

block off the trap with soil. Only one (four-day) attempt was made to catch any particular mole and the traps were used for one treatment only in order to avoid cross-contamination of odours.

The results of the experimental trapping were quite unambiguous: the traps treated with weasel odour or with 2,2-dimethylthietane were markedly less efficient at catching moles than were the clean traps, while adding oil of peppermint appeared, thank heavens, to have no discernible effect (Table 7.1). One can conclude, with some confidence, that moles avoid both natural weasel scent and synthetic dimethylthietane.

Our confidence boosted by these results, we then went on to carry out a field trial designed to determine whether or not moles will avoid tunnels that have been treated with predator odours. For this experiment a very special mole was chosen, one which, from the pattern of its molehills, appeared to have a territory consisting of two main areas connected by a narrow strip of raised, dry land passing between wet, boggy depressions. The mole, an adult male, was caught in December and equipped with a radio transmitter. It was then released and its movements recorded over the next six days. We were unable to follow the animal continuously over this period. Instead, on each of the six days the animal was followed throughout just one of its three activity periods, advancing one period on each consecutive day.

On the seventh day of the experiment, while the mole was fast asleep in its nest, a total of 30 clean cigarette filters were placed into the tunnels connecting the two parts of the territory and at various points scattered throughout the upper part. The filters were introduced through small holes made with a sharp probe in the roofs of the tunnels and then carefully sealed with soil. This procedure was the control for the next part of the experiment when we would use similar filters to slowly release the odorous compounds. The movements of the mole were then followed for a further three days.

At the end of this control period a further 30 filters were placed into the tunnels at approximately the same positions as the previous 30. However, this time the filters had been soaked in 2,2-dimethylthietane. The mole was then followed yet again until, eight days later, the radio failed and the experiment was at an end.

The radio-tracking confirmed that our interpretation of the pattern of molehills was correct and that the mole did indeed have a range consisting of two main areas which were connected by, as far as could be determined, just three tunnels, and with a single nest in the lower part of the territory (Figure 7.2, top). In this three-dimensional figure the vertical component reflects the number of times the animal was located

Figure 7.2 An experiment into repelling moles. Three-dimensional representations of the use made by a mole of different parts of its range. The plots were made by dividing the map into a matrix of 25 m² and counting the number of times the mole was located in each. The maps are drawn as if viewed from the south-east with the observation point situated 10,000 map units from the centre of the matrix and 20° above the horizontal.

The upper map shows how the range was used prior to the experiment, the middle map shows the situation following the introduction of control stimuli, and the lower map the result of introducing dimethylthietane into the tunnels. See text for further details

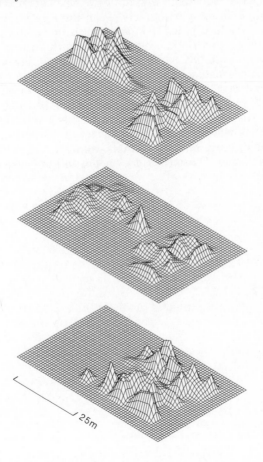

in different parts of the territory. Clearly, during the initial six-day period the mole was using all parts of his range more or less equally and he continued to do so after the introduction of the clean, control cigarette filters (Figure 7.2, middle). However, once the filters treated with the synthetic predator scent had been placed in the tunnels the mole ceased to forage in the upper, treated area, and began to expand the network of tunnels in the lower part of his range (Figure 7.3, bottom).

'Eureka!' we hear you cry. It does indeed seem that moles are, to some degree at least, repelled not only by the conspecific odours discussed earlier but also by those produced by mustelid carnivores. However, before rushing off to the Patents Office, we must ask some hard questions

111

about whether these substances are likely to be of practical use in mole control in the real world. In general we fear that the answer must be no. They may have a minor role to play in deterring moles from small, high-amenity areas, such as lawns, where the gardener is unwilling to apply more robust measures and where his or her labour comes free. On any larger scale of operation serious difficulties and problems begin to arise. To begin with, the labour and material costs of treating large areas of tunnels would be high, particularly given the relatively minor costs of mole damage in the first place. To make matters worse the chemicals in question are highly volatile and even if incorporated into a slow-release formulation they would have to be renewed on a regular basis. Mammals are very versatile beasts and if the substances were to be used to treat large areas then it is very likely that the moles, faced with noxious stimuli in all directions, would quickly become habituated to them, that is to say they would simply ignore them. There is also the very real danger that moles would simply block off any treated tunnels, and that the subsequent digging of new tunnels would exacerbate rather than improve the situation. Overall, it does seem to be a case of back to the drawing-board!

8 Swimming for a living

The desmans live such very different lives from moles that they have been left to be dealt with separately.

DISTRIBUTION AND HABITAT PREFERENCE

During the Pleistocene *Desmana moschata* ranged right across Europe, in a broad band from southern Britain in the west to the Caspian Sea in the east. Since those ancient times the species has become progressively more and more restricted in distribution, so much so that by historical times it was confined to the southern part of European Russia, to the basins of the rivers Dnieper, Don, Kama, Ural and Volga and to a few small rivers, such as the Mius, which flow into the Sea of Azov.

Galemys pyrenaicus is known only from Quaternary deposits associated with the Pyrenees and their foothills. However, its fossil remains are easily overlooked and its distribution was probably much wider than these discoveries indicate. Today, the species is restricted in distribution to the northern half of the Iberian peninsula and to the French side of the Pyrenees.

Although both of the living species of desmans are clearly adapted for a semi-aquatic life, nevertheless their specific habitat requirements are very different indeed. The Russian desman avoids rapid currents and seems to prefer low-lying oxbow lakes and river pools which are slow flowing and even stagnant. The heavy, dank atmosphere of the haunts favoured by the desman along the valley of the River Kerzhenets is clearly evoked in the writings of A. N. Formozov (quoted in Ognev, 1928).

> The desman usually stays strictly in the shallow lakes of the floodlands. These parts, which are vestiges of the changing course of the Kerzhenets are seldom wider than 10–25 sagenes [1 sagene=2.13 m], and they are of elongated appearance and frequently of bizarre form (from which they derive their names of Kalachik [pretzel], Kosti [bones] etc.). A large quantity of flood debris such as treetrunks, twigs, and half-rotten leaves and needles are deposited each spring on the bottom and vegetation, alders and

113

willow shrubs encroaching from the shore into the shallow lake grow on the moisture permeated soil. Half submerged black alder forests in which the trees grow, as it were, on enormous tussocks of earth are especially characteristic for the animal. Numerous streams meander among these tussocks where reeds, cattails and sedges proliferate and where, in the spring, lovely yellow irises grow. In some areas semi-liquid and quaking moss carpets are very numerous. The water of these forest ponds is of a brownish colour, not very clear, with a strong smell of decomposing vegetable matter. It is in such conditions that the natural habitations of the desman in the lakes of the Kerzhenets floodlands can be found.

The world occupied by the Pyrenean desman could hardly be more different. Whilst *Desmana* positively abhors swiftly running waters, *Galemys* seems to take delight in plunging into the wildest of mountain torrents (Plates 7 & 8). This species enjoys a high-altitude distribution and can be found near the sources of major rivers at elevations of well over 2,500 m. At the lower end of its altitudinal range it is rarely found below 400 m except, perhaps, in the Basque country. Between these upper and lower altitudinal limits the species frequents clear, unpolluted and fast-flowing streams and really comes into its own in lively and highly oxygenated mountain torrents. According to Richard (1985) the ideal habitat for the Pyrenean desman is a torrential stream flowing through meadows, bordered by boulders and drystone walls, and lined with open-canopied trees, such as ash and alder, which do not cast too intense a shade across the water. The stones of the stream bank together with the exposed roots of the trees provide good shelter while the light ensures an abundance of plant life for the aquatic invertebrates on which the desman feeds. The desman is usually absent from areas which have been planted with coniferous trees largely because they block out most of the light, but also because their cast needles acidify both the soil and the water.

THE HOME BASE

Desmans, like moles, usually have a single nest site to which they return in order to sleep and rest. The Pyrenean desman does not dig a burrow but instead makes use of one of the multitude of natural shelters provided by the rocks and roots bordering the mountain streams along which it lives. The drystone walls built immediately alongside the banks of some streams by farmers make particularly desirable residences for desmans. The entrance to the nest site almost always lies underwater and leads upwards to a circular nest chamber some 15 cm in diameter. If the animal should feel the need to improve its shelter by rearranging the sand or soil that lies among the rocks, then it will do so with its proboscis-like snout, rather than with its feet. Richard (1985) suggests that this is because the claws of the feet are essential for gripping onto the rocks and resisting the torrential flow of water. If the desman is not to be swept away when it is out and about, then the claws must be kept sharp and in pristine condition. The desman may further improve its home comforts by

Figure 8.1 The burrow systems of Russian desmans (after Barabasch-Nikiforow, 1975)

collecting moss, twigs and leaves in order to make a nest. The fact that the Pyrenean desman can survive the intense cold of winter in such rudimentary shelters testifies to the high quality of its fur. This consists of three layers: a fine, waterproof and down-like underfur, a middle layer of pile hairs, and a sparse covering of long oily guard hairs.

Russian desmans are much more enthusiastic excavators than their Pyrenean cousins, and they dig themselves a proper burrow in the soft shore of their pond, stream or creek. Usually, but by no means always, there is a single entrance which opens underwater and at such a depth that it remains navigable even when the surface of the water freezes. Desmans do not hibernate but continue to forage under the ice throughout the winter.

The burrow leads eventually to a nest which is almost always placed near to the surface of the ground, in loose soil, among the roots of a tree or bush. The length of the burrow is determined by the distance from the shoreline to the nearest trees or shrubs; if the shore is gently sloping the burrow tends to be long, whereas if it is steep the burrow is short (Figure 8.1). Because of its location, near to the surface and in soil that is fissured by a network of roots, the nest is well ventilated despite the fact that its entrance lies underwater for much of the year. The nest itself is made up of sedge leaves and mosses collected from the shore tussocks and from decaying trees. A notable feature of the nest site is that it is often awfully smelly and littered with discarded fish bones.

The nest of the Russian desman is usually built well above the highest level of water to be expected during the summer months. However, if the snow melt in the spring is unusually rapid the nest may become inundated and then the desman may be forced to abandon its home temporarily. It is at such times that desmans are most likely to be seen during the hours of daylight, as they perch on what high ground they can find, looking thoroughly despondent and waiting for the waters to recede. It is in such circumstances that they are also most vulnerable, not only to the attentions of man, who hunts them for their lustrous fine fur, but to

Figure 8.2 Annual changes in the size of a population of Russian desmans (based on data in Barabasch-Nikiforow, 1975)

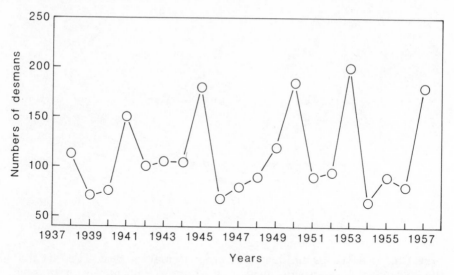

birds of prey such as reed-harriers, black kites and ospreys. At least one unlucky individual is known to have fallen foul of both bird and man! The following extract by N. A. Zarudnyi (quoted in Ognev, 1928) will explain.

> In April 1887, seeing an osprey near the junction of the Sakmara and Ural circling high over the flood, I approached it within gunshot range. The bird just then dived into the water, caught a black animal of some kind and passed overhead. A successful shot gave me two acquisitions at once — the hawk and the desman.

A rapid spring thaw, therefore, brings both inconvenience and some degree of danger. An unexpected thaw in midwinter is another matter altogether; this is a much more serious affair and can prove to be quite disastrous to large numbers of desmans. The problem is that during a winter thaw the thick ice can remain intact and firmly attached to the shoreline. The rains and melting snows then rapidly flood both the ice and the surrounding land to such a depth that the desmans become trapped in their flooded nests and without the strength to break through the ice, or the time to dig through the soil to the surface, they drown. Such unseasonable flooding can have a very profound and prolonged impact on the demography of a local population of desmans. One result is that populations tend to vary quite considerably in size from year to year (Figure 8.2). This is, of course, in stark contrast to the situation with moles, which live in a generally stable and dependable environment and whose populations fluctuate in size only within very narrow limits. However, winter flooding is only one of the factors involved in inducing population fluctuations in the Russian desman; changes in population size also depend to a large extent on annual variations in rainfall and consequent water levels. This is clearly shown by data collected in the

Figure 8.3 The relationship between rainfall and the numbers of desmans present in the Oka Reserve during the summer (based on data in Borodin, 1963)

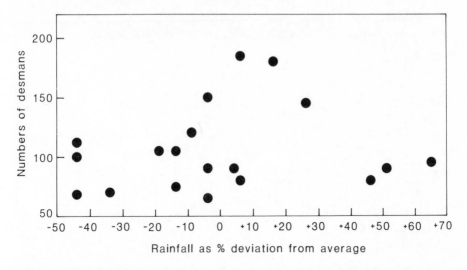

Oka Nature Reserve (Borodin, 1963; Figure 8.3). In this region summer densities of desmans tend to be highest in those years when rainfall and spring water levels have been of average magnitude. In years when water levels are unusually low the areas available for feeding are much reduced and, as a result, breeding success is poor. Conversely, in years of particularly heavy precipitation and high water levels, many animals are drowned or are forced out of the area because they cannot find a nest site; again the result is a relatively low population density.

FOOD AND FORAGING

The food of both species of desmans consists of a wide variety of relatively small aquatic life.

The Russian desman is largely nocturnal in its habits and is rarely seen during the hours of daylight except on those occasions when it has been flooded out of its nest. Babuschkin (1967a) has been able to show, by regular counts of the numbers of individuals seen to be actively feeding near the centre of a lake, that desmans forage throughout the night but with peaks of increased activity at dusk and dawn (Figure 8.4). The diet of *Desmana* includes insect larvae, worms and leeches, molluscs, small fishes and frogs, and their eggs. The relative importance of the different prey types varies considerably throughout the year, depending upon what happens to be 'in season' at any given time (Figure 8.5). Rather surprisingly, quantities of plant life are consumed at all times of the year; A. N. Formozov (quoted in Ognev, 1928) described how desmans often come to the surface at sunrise and sunset to chew on the white roots of an unidentified water-plant until their stomachs are rendered quite taut with finely chewed vegetable matter.

Figure 8.4 Russian desmans are nocturnal: numbers of individuals foraging near the centre of a lake at different times (based on data in Babuschkin, 1967a)

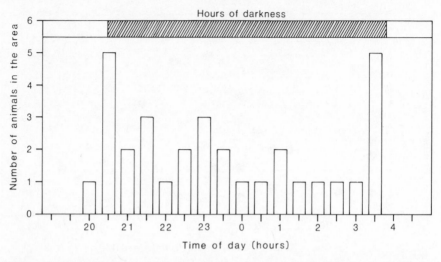

Figure 8.5 Seasonal changes in the diet of the Russian desman (after Barabasch-Nikiforow, 1975)

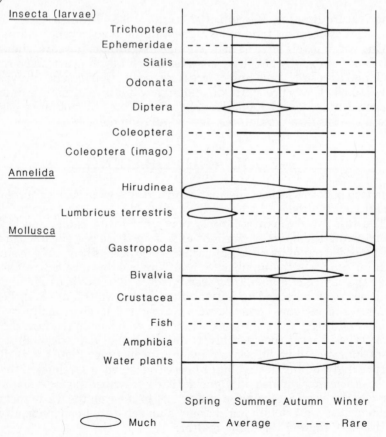

Figure 8.6 The patterns of activity of two pairs of Pyrenean desmans. The stippled areas represent the hours of darkness (after Stone & Gorman, 1985)

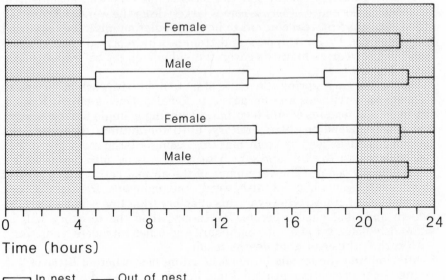

Time (hours)

▭ In nest   —— Out of nest

When actively foraging, *Desmana* relies much more on smell and touch than sight. While swimming at the surface, the proboscis-like snout is often held above the water, like the periscope of a submarine, constantly testing the air for signs of prey or danger. When foraging underwater the creature swims along, just above the bottom, constantly turning its agile snout from side and side and frequently darting it into the slime to extract an item of prey which is then transferred to the mouth to be bolted, often underwater, whole or in large chunks.

The Pyrenean desman is also a predominantly nocturnal species although, in May and July at least, individuals are often also active for a short time during each afternoon (Figure 8.6). The diet of *Galemys* reflects, naturally enough, what food is present in montane streams and thus consists largely of aquatic insects and their larvae, particularly Trichoptera (caddis-flies), Ephemeroptera (mayflies) and Plecoptera (stone-flies), together with freshwater gammarid shrimps and small molluscs. The amount of food available in these mountain streams can be surprisingly high; in a good Pyrenean torrent, four metres wide, the drift of arthropods out of the substrate and into the water column can exceed 0.5 kg per metre per day (Richard, 1985). The Pyrenean desman obtains its food by diving into the torrent to thrust and probe among the rocks and gravel with its prehensile snout. The proboscis is kept in a state of constant and excited agitation, lightly brushing across and sniffing at any interesting object that the desman encounters. The snout is so incredibly adept at grasping and immobilising objects, and then transferring them to the mouth, that any item of prey that is discovered stands very little chance indeed of escape.

SOCIAL BEHAVIOUR AND REPRODUCTION

The social behaviour of Russian desmans is not very well documented; what little information there is comes largely from the work of Krazovski (1954), but the first real clues as to how a population might be organised were provided by fur trappers and traders who reported that at some times of the year as many as seven individuals might be scared from a single burrow.

During the early spring the males start to fight with each other and to compete for territories and for access to females. Once a pair is formed, the male and female remain together, occupying a single burrow system and jointly defending their territory, until the autumn. Tenure of the territory is advertised by scent marking, using a large scent gland that lies underneath the tail and which secretes a dense oily liquid with a strong musky odour. (The very name of the animal betrays its powerful smell: both *desman*, a Swedish word, and *moschata* from the Greek *moskhos*, mean musk.) However, this olfactory front line is but a warning system and, if it should become necessary, then the territory will be vigorously defended against neighbours and other intruders, sometimes with such enthusiasm that deaths result.

After mating the female builds a breeding nest where a litter of 3–5 young is born sometime around June. For the first few days after birth the female stays with the young but then she builds a nest of her own, within the same burrow system, and thereafter visits the young only in order to suckle them. The male also takes an active interest in the young and often shares their nest and thus helps keep them warm. After weaning the young remain with their parents and forage within the family's territory for the rest of the summer; this is the time at which several individuals can be trapped at a single burrow. By the time autumn arrives the young are fully grown and independent and are beginning to disperse away from their natal area. They usually disperse overland, rather than by water; in this way they minimise their chances of an encounter with a territorial adult, but at the expense of an increased risk of attack from predators. Once the young have gone, the bond between the parents rapidly breaks down and they separate. Whether the members of a breeding pair get together again in future years, or whether they prefer to seek out new partners, is unknown.

Lamentably little is known about the breeding biology of the Pyrenean desman. Pregnant females are first encountered in late January of any year and there are three clear peaks in the proportion of pregnant females in a population; one in February, one in mid-March and one in mid-May. This, together with the fact that pregnant females are frequently found to be in a state of full lactation, suggests that most females give birth to two or more litters per year. There is little information on litter size, but in trapped and dissected females the most common number of embryos is four. It is likely that both sexes first breed when they are twelve months old and do so in each subsequent year until they die. From an examination of tooth wear in a sample of 87 skulls, Richard (1985) has estimated that few animals live beyond their third year, a lifespan that is similar to that of moles.

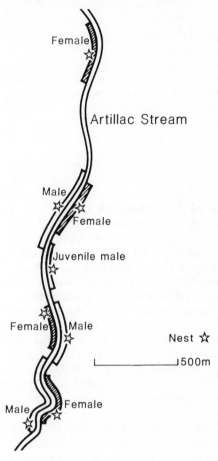

Figure 8.7 The spatial organisation of Pyrenean desmans living along the Artillac stream in the French Pyrenees. For the sake of clarity the ranges of an individual are shown along one bank only; in reality each animal used both banks and the full width of the stream (after Stone & Gorman, 1985)

The social organisation of the Pyrenean desman has been investigated in some depth, at least during the summer months (Stone & Gorman, 1985, Stone 1985). These studies, which involved fitting desmans with radio transmitters, were carried out along a number of streams in the Ariège region of the French Pyrenees during the months of May, June and July.

Once they have established themselves in an area along a stream, adult desmans probably remain there for the rest of their lives. In the Ariège region the population consisted, in the main, of pairs of animals of opposite sex each living in a jointly occupied linear range, but with each animal having its own nest (Figure 8.7). Generally, the female of each pair occupied a relatively short range (mean$=301\pm7$ m; n$=7$), centrally enclosed within the longer range of her mate (mean$=429\pm10$ m; n$=7$). At their extremities the ranges of males overlapped to a relatively small degree with those of their neighbours, the average length of disputed ground amounting to around 7 per cent of the range. The disputed areas between neighbouring ranges were extremely attractive to the males, who spent a disproportionate amount of their active time patrolling in them as compared to the central areas of their territories (Figure 8.8). When in these contested border areas the males fed little, if at all, but instead spent their time swimming to and fro across the stream, carefully examining all the rocks and the banks and frequently pausing to scent mark with their sub-caudal glands. It would seem, therefore, that males are territorial and that they do everything in their power to prevent other males from gaining access to their females. The ranges of the females, enclosed as they were within those of their partners, overlapped not at all with those of their neighbours and, in contrast to their male partners, the females concentrated their activities towards the central parts of their ranges (Figure 8.8).

In addition to the established breeding pairs, the area also contained

Figure 8.8 The proportion of time that three pairs of male and female Pyrenean desmans spent in different parts of their ranges (after Stone, 1985)

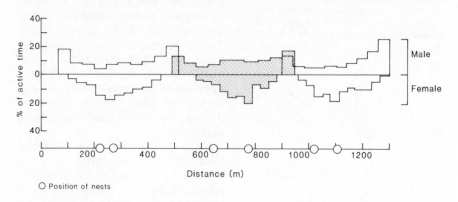

O Position of nests

solitary individuals, some of them the young of the year, others adults. It seems likely that these were transitory individuals who had yet to acquire a territory or mate and who were currently moving through the area. One of them, for example, was observed to travel over 2.7 km during a single activity period. This probably explains the very high number of individuals that can be trapped on some streams; there is, for example, an authentic record of 79 desmans being trapped on a 3 km stretch of river during the course a single year. Undoubtedly the majority of these animals would have been transient individuals rather than permanent residents.

Despite the fact that the territories of males overlap, albeit to a small extent, neighbours rarely came into contact with each other. This is just as well, because desmans are highly intolerant of their own kind and will fight quite ferociously if they meet. In order to understand how such bloody encounters are avoided, an appreciation of the daily pattern of activity is required.

During the summer months the desmans in the Ariège displayed two distinct periods of activity in each 24 hours; one at night and a shorter one during the afternoon (Figure 8.6). The activity periods of neighbouring pairs of desmans were highly synchronised with each other; for example, on one stream daylight activity started between 1 and 1.30 p.m. and all the residents were actively foraging by 1.45. During any one activity period both the male and the female of a pair moved either upstream or downstream, although they foraged separately and at some distance from each other (Figure 8.9). Furthermore, they both moved upstream from their nests in one active period and downstream in the next, and in this way they routinely covered the whole of their territory every 24 hours.

This is the clue as to how neighbours avoid meeting in areas of overlap. On any given stretch of stream all the desmans moved upstream in one activity period and all moved downstream in the next, as shown by three neighbouring pairs living along the Bouigane stream (Figure 8.9).

Figure 8.9 The movements of three pairs of Pyrenean desmans over a period of 24 hours. Note the synchrony of activity between the pairs, and the fact that all the animals move up or downstream at the same times

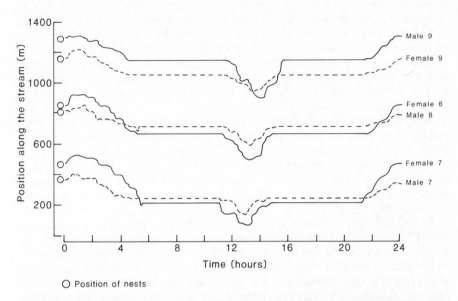

O Position of nests

Thus in Pyrenean desmans, as in moles, overt and potentially deadly confrontation between neighbours is avoided by temporal isolation, with only one individual using jointly held areas, be it stream or ground, at any given time.

CONSERVATION AND PROGNOSIS

Quite clearly, as a group the desmans are not one of life's great success stories. They have never been a very diverse group and the two species that are still with us are now very much restricted and fragmented in distribution and must be regarded as prime candidates for extinction. This sad state of affairs has probably resulted primarily from the desmans' high degree of specialisation for a life in habitats which are quite rare, which are discontinuous, and which are unusually sensitive to climatic changes. The particularly severe vicissitudes of climate that characterised the Pleistocene must have led to the local extinction of desmans on a large scale. Those populations that managed to survive the last ice age found themselves isolated on watery islands of wetland set in a dry sea of habitats in which they could not survive and which they could cross with only the very greatest of difficulty. These populations would have been small and genetically isolated and thus highly susceptible to the problems of inbreeding, and particularly prone to extinction as a result of such random visitations as disease and famine. The chances of any vanished population being subsequently replaced by recolonisation from elsewhere would have been remote. Thus the gradual decline in the fortunes of desmans has been due, largely, to natural climatic changes and to the consequent loss and fragmentation of suitable habitat. In addition, thanks to the activities of man, the problems facing desmans have multiplied and have become much more intense over the last century or so.

The Pyrenean desman faces challenges on several fronts. The number of highly productive mountain torrents available to desmans decreases year by year as a result of dam projects and road building. Invertebrate populations are adversely affected by pollution from agro-chemicals, road salt and acid rain, by the planting of conifers which block out the light, and by deforestation at higher altitudes which leads to soil erosion and to the scouring of the stream beds.

Galemys also suffers from misguided persecution, on the one hand from anglers who imagine that it eats a lot of young fish, and on the other from over-enthusiastic museum collectors. Poduschka & Richard (1986) have reported seeing 70 recently collected skins in the laboratory of a university professor in Madrid, despite the fact that the species enjoys legal protection in Spain and that the scholar in question did not even work on the species!

A new and quite devastating threat to the survival of the desman in Spain has recently emerged. Some 30 years ago a commercial mink farm was established at El Espinar 130 km from Madrid. Inevitably, a number of mink have escaped over the years and this alien, semi-aquatic predator is now firmly established in the wild. Desmans stand no chance at all against this highly opportunistic killer and they have already disappeared from areas where they were formerly abundant. The prospects for the survival of the desman in areas where mink abound are bleak indeed.

The Russian desman has long been hunted for its lustrous fur, which is prized for being extremely soft and dense. Originally, the furs were taken only for local use and the desman remained a common species in many parts of its range. However, during the latter part of the nineteenth century a regular commercial export trade in its skins became established and hunting pressures dramatically intensified. There are, for example, records from Nizhini Novgorod of villagers bringing 400–500 pelts to market on a single day (Ognev, 1928). With this level of exploitation the numbers of desmans declined sharply in many areas.

The methods used to kill desmans varied from place to place and from season to season. The people of Ryazan province had a pretty straightforward approach to the problem: one hunter would scare an animal out of its burrow and his companion would club it to death as it emerged. As we have said above, in April and May desmans are often flooded out of their homes and obliged to seek shelter among tree roots on high ground. Hunters would ambush them at such times and shoot them as they emerged to feed at dusk. Up to 1890 the Kerzhenets floodlands were densely populated with desmans as no one hunted them. Later on, however, the heavy demand for pelts led to widespread hunting, usually with snares or creels placed underwater at the entrance to the burrow. Shooting was less common and took place early on in the year as the ice began to melt. Two hunters would work together in a dugout canoe, lurking among the trees until they spotted a feeding desman. The man in the back of the boat would then row after the animal, following its movements along the bottom of the lake by the trail of bubbles rising to the surface. Eventually the desman would surface for air, only to be shot by the marksman in the bow. Prior to the First World War a skilled pair of hunters could get 40 pelts in a month by this method.

Commercial hunting declined considerably during the First World War and the early years of the Revolution, and the overexploited populations were able to recover to some extent. Unfortunately the furs remained in demand and hunting was soon resumed to the continuing detriment of the species.

In more recent years hunting has become less of a threat but it has been replaced by a number of other, all to familiar, problems of the modern world. Large areas of the wetland haunts of the desman have been drained for agriculture, leading to further fragmentation and isolation of populations and to reductions in their density. The desman also now faces competition for space from two introduced aquatic rodents, the coypu, *Myocastor coypus*, and the muskrat, *Ondata zibethicus*. Both of these species are native to the New World but escapees from fur farms have established themselves in wetlands in various parts of Europe. To make matters yet worse for the desman, pollution from industry and agriculture is as rife in the region as it is elsewhere in the developed world. One can only hope that, despite such formidable problems, this charming and totally inoffensive creature will continue to thrive in those few areas where it still exists. The desmans have been left to the closing pages of this book; let us hope that our generation is not to have the dubious honour of witnessing the last chapter of their very existence.

Appendix I:
Keeping moles in captivity

Without specialised equipment it is very difficult indeed to study the behaviour of free-living moles. Happily, it is quite easy to keep moles in captivity where they can be readily observed. They soon get used to being handled and can make gentle and fascinating, if somewhat demanding, pets.

OBTAINING YOUR MOLE

Probably, the simplest way to catch moles is to unearth them when they are digging shallow surface tunnels. All that is required is patience, quick reflexes, and a spade or fork. Having discovered an actively digging mole, one creeps up on it and then rapidly digs a heel into the tunnel behind it so as to prevent it escaping back down the tunnel. The mole can then be turned out onto the surface of the ground with a quick flick of the spade. A newly caught mole is best picked up by the tail, swung gently onto a flat surface, and grasped around the body behind the front legs. In this way the mole's somewhat painful bite can be avoided.

HOUSING YOUR MOLE

If a mole is to be kept for only a few days then a small container, such as a bucket, will suffice as accommodation. About 20 cm of damp, friable soil should be placed in the bottom of the container and renewed every few days. Some workers have used sawdust as a substitute but it appears that moles really do need to dig and move through soil if they are to maintain their fur in good condition. A quantity of dry hay should be provided so that it can make a nest. Since moles are quite good climbers, the container should be covered with wire mesh so as to prevent escape while providing good ventilation.

In general, moles should be housed singly, otherwise they will kill one another. That having been said, Henning (1957), says that *Scalopus aquaticus* can be kept in pairs of the same, or opposite, sex.

If you want to keep a mole for a longer period, then rather larger quarters will need to be provided. Redfern & Mitchell (1987) have

Figure AI.1 Details of the construction of a mole accommodation unit

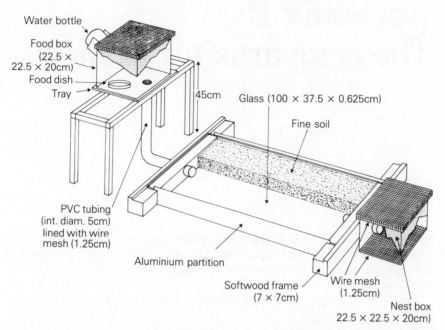

described a 'state of the art' habitation in which they have housed European moles for up to 443 days, with a mean survival time of 268 days. The details of the construction, which provides separate sleeping, activity and eating areas, are shown in Figure AI.1.

The nest box, filled with hay, was made from 10 mm plywood with a 1.25 cm 'Weldmesh' floor and removable lid, and was connected to the activity area by a 15 cm length of 5 cm PVC tubing.

The activity area consisted of a softwood and aluminium-sheet frame placed on a solid floor. It was filled to a depth of 7 cm with fine light soil and covered with a sheet of 6 mm plate glass.

The food-box, which rested on a shallow tray, was made of 20 gauge sheet aluminium with a removable cover of 1.25 cm 'Weldmesh'. The tunnel leading from the activity area to the feeding box was lined with 1.25 cm 'Weldmesh' to provide footholds for the mole.

The moles usually defecated in the soil but if it was raked over once a week it remained fresh for several months. In hot weather, it was necessary to keep the soil damp with an occasional light watering.

FEEDING YOUR MOLE

Moles do best when fed on earthworms, particularly large species such as *Lumbricus terrestris*, and every effort should be made to include them in the diet. Luckily, they will also take a variety of other food which can be obtained with rather less effort, such as tinned dog-food, minced ox heart, chopped lamb's liver and, if available, freshly dead, hairless, mouse or rat nestlings.

Appendix II:
The ectoparasites of moles

Moles, like all other mammals, suffer from a variety of ectoparasites. Our knowledge of these pests is rudimentary, with the exception of those of the European mole and the New World moles, which are quite well documented.

The following fleas have been recorded from the European mole:

Palaeopsylla minor
Palaeopsylla kohauti
Ctenophthalmus bisoctodentatus
Ctenophthalmus nobilis
Hystrichopsylla talpae
Rectofrontia pentacantha

The fur mite *Labidophorus soricis* and the tick *Ixodes hexagonus* are also often present. Godfrey & Crowcroft (1960) give a long list of species of mites which have been found associated with this mole or its nest. In the case of most of them it is unclear whether there is a real ecological relationship between mite and mole. Many are probably soil species which have strayed, accidentally, into mole nests.

Yates *et al.* (1979) have identified the ectoparasites from a large number of New World moles captured at sites throughout the USA and western Canada. These are listed in Table AII.1.

A notable feature of many of these species is that they are not host-specific to moles, but are also found on a variety of other small mammals. The utilisation of mole tunnels by other species is well known and probably results in ready cross-infestation. For example, Eadie (1939) caught *Blarina brevicauda*, *Microtus pennsylvanicus*, *Peromyscus leucopus*, *Sorex cinereus*, *Pitymys pinetorum*, *Synaptomys cooperi*, *Condylura cristata* and *Zapus hudsonius* in tunnels that had been dug by *Parascalops breweri*.

Table AII.1 Ectoparasites of North American moles.

PARASITE	HOSTS
Lice (Anoplura)	
Haematopinoides squamosus	1.
Fleas (Siphonaptera)	
Ctenophthalmus pseudagyrtes	1,5.
Corypsylla jordani	2,7.
Corypsylla ornata	2,3,4,5,7.
Nearctopsylla jordani	3,4.
Catallagia decipiens	3.
Epitedia scapani	7.
Beetles (Coleoptera)	
Leptinus testaceus	1.
Mites (Acari)	
Ixodes angustus	2,3,4,7.
Hirstionyssus blarinae	3,4,5.
Androlaelaps fahrenholzi	1,2,4,5,6,7.
Haemogamasus keegani	2.
Haemogamasus reidi	1.
Haemogamasus liponyssoides	2,3,4,5.
Neotrombicula brennani	4.

KEY TO HOSTS
1. *Parascalops breweri*
2. *Scapanus latimanus*
3. *Scapanus orarius*
4. *Scapanus townsendii*
5. *Scalopus aquaticus*
6. *Condylura cristata*
7. *Neurotrichus gibbsii*

Postscript:
A Want Catcher's Epitaph

He wanted all his life
and yet by Wanting
His wants were all supplied,
and when he Wanted more
He wanted less,
and when he Wanted least he died.

(Swanton, 1938)

References

Adams, L.E. (1903) 'A contribution to our knowledge of the mole (*Talpa europaea* L.)', *Mem. Proc. Manchr. Lit. Phil. Soc.*, 47(4), 1–39

Arena, J.M. (1974) *Poisoning, Toxicology, Symptoms, Treatments*, Charles C. Thomas, Illinois

Arlton, A.V. (1936) 'An ecological study of the mole', *J. Mammal.*, 17, 349–371

Armsby, A. (1952) *Moles*, West Norfolk Newspapers Ltd

Babuschkin, G.M. (1967a) *Infrakrasyne luci i provedenie zivotnych. Priroda*, H, 7

—— (1967b) 'O faktorach ogranicivajuscich cislennost' vychucholi', *Sovesc. po probleme ochrany vychucholi.* Vortragsthesen, Woronesh

Balli, A. (1940) 'Observazioni biologiche su *Talpa europaea*', *Riv. Biol.*, 29, 35–54

Barabasch-Nikiforow, I.I. (1975) *Die Desmane*, A. Ziemsen Verlag, Wittenberg

Barrett-Hamilton, S.E.H. (1910) *A History of British Mammals*, 2 vols., Gurney and Jackson, London

Bashkirov, I.S. & Zharkov, I.V. (1934) 'On the biology of the mole in Tartary', *Uchen, Zap. Kazan. Univ.*, 94, 1–66

Bateman, J.A. (1959) 'Laboratory studies of the golden mole and the mole-rat', *African Wildlife*, 13, 65–71

Becker, K. (1959) 'Uber einen spatwurf bei *Talpa europaea* L.', *Z. Saugetierk.*, 24, 93–95

Boonstra, R. & Krebs, C.J. (1977) 'A fencing experiment on a high-density population of *Microtus townsendii*', *Can J. Zool.*, 55, 1166–1175

Borodin, L.P. (1963) *Russkaja vychuchol'*. Saransk.

Corbet, G.B. & Hill, J.E. (1986) *A World List of Mammalian Species*, Second Edition, British Museum (Natural History), London

Corbet, G.B. & Ovenden, D. (1980) *The Mammals of Britain and Europe*, Collins, London

Deansley, R. (1966) 'Observations on reproduction in the mole (*Talpa europaea*)', *Symp. Zool. Soc. Lond.*, 15, 387–402

Dixon, K.R. & Chapman, J.A. (1980) 'Harmonic mean measures of animal activity centres', *Ecology*, 61, 1040–1044

Eadie, W.R. (1939) 'A contribution to the biology of *Parascalops breweri*', *J. Mammal.*, 20, 150–173

Eadie, W.R. & Hamilton, W.J. Jr (1956) 'Notes on reproduction in the star-nosed mole', *J. Mammal.*, 37, 223–231

Evans A.C. (1948) 'The identity of earthworms stored by moles', *Proc. Zool. Soc. Lond.*, 118, 356–359

Farlow, J.O. (1976) 'A consideration of the trophic dynamics of a late Cretaceous large-dinosaur community (Oldman Formation)', *Ecology*, 57, 841–857

Funmilayo, O. (1979) 'Food consumption, preferences and storage in the mole', *Acta Theriol.*, 25, 379–389

Gasc, J.P., Jouffroy, F.K., Renous, S. & von Bloonitz, F. (1986) 'Morphofunctional study of the digging system of the Namib Desert golden mole *Eremitalpa granti namibensis*; cinefluorographical and anatomical analysis', *J. Zool., Lond.*, 208, 9–36

Giger, R.D. (1965) 'The surface activity of moles as indicated in barn owl pellets', *Murrelet* 46, 32–36

Godet, R. (1951) 'Contribution à l'ethologie de la taupe (*Talpa europaea* L.)', *Bull. Soc. Zool. Fr.*, 76, 107–128

Godfrey, G.K. (1955) 'A field study of the activity of the mole (*T. europaea* L.)', *Ecology*, 36, 678–685

—— (1956) 'Reproduction of *Talpa europaea* in Suffolk', *J. Mammal.*, 37, 438–440

—— (1957a) 'Observations on the movements of moles (*T. europaea*, L.) after weaning', *Proc. Zool. Soc. Lond.*, 128, 287–295

—— (1957b) 'Aggressive behaviour in the mole, *T. europaea* L.', *Proc. Zool. Soc. Lond.*, 128, 602–604

Godfrey, G.K. & Crowcroft, P. (1960) *The Life of the Mole (T. europaea Linnaeus)*, Museum press, London

Gorman, M.L. (1984) 'The response of prey to stoat (*Mustela erminea*) scent', *J. Zool., Lond.*, 202, 419–423

Gorman, M.L. & Stone, R.D. (in press) 'Repelling moles' in R. Putman (ed.), *Mammals as Pests, Chapman and Hall*, London

Grue, H. & Jensen, B. (1979) 'Review of the formation of incremental lines in tooth cementum of terrestrial mammals', *Danish Rev. Game Biol.*, 11(3), 1–48

Guy, W.A. (1868) *Principles of Forensic Medicine*, Henry Renshaw, London

Haeck J. (1969) 'Colonisation of the mole (*T. europaea*, L) in the Ijsselmeerpolders', *Neth. J. Zool.*, 19(2), 145–248

Hall, E.R. (1981) *Mammals of North America*, Second Edition, John Wiley and Sons, New York

Hallett, J.G. (1978) '*Parascalops breweri*', *Mammalian Species*, 98, 1–4, American Society of Mammalogists

Hamilton, W.J. Jr. (1931) 'Habits of the star-nosed mole *Condylura cristata*', *J. Mammal.*, 12, 345–355

Hartman, G.D. & Yates, T.L. (1985) '*Scapanus orarius*', *Mammalian Species*, 253, 1–5, American Society of Mammalogists

Hawes, M.L. (1975) 'Odour as a possible isolating mechanism in sympatric species of shrews (*Sorex vagrans* and *S. obscurus*)', *J. Mammal.*, 57, 404–406

Heck, L. (1912) *Die Saugetiere*, Alfred Brehm, Leipzig

Hemmingsen, A.M. (1960) 'Energy metabolism as related to body size and respiratory surfaces, and its evolution', *Reports of the Steno Memorial Hospital and Nordinsk Insulin Laboratorium*, 9, 6–110

Henning, W.L. (1957) 'The eastern prairie mole (*Scalopus aquaticus machrinus* Rafinesque)', in Warden & Lane-Petter (eds.), *The UFAW Handbook*, UFAW, London

Hickman, G.C. (1982) 'Climbing ability of the star-nosed mole, *Condylura cristata* (Talpidae)', *Saugetierkdl. Mitt.*, 40, 296–297

—— (1986) 'Swimming of *Amblysomus hottentotus* (Insectivora: Chrysochloridae), with notes on *Chrysospalax* and *Eremitalpa*', *Cimbebasia (A)*, 8(7), 55–61

—— (1988) 'The swimming ability of *Ctenomys fulvus* (Ctenomydidae) and *Spalacopus cyanus* (Octodontidae), with reference to swimming in other subterranean mammals', *Z. Saugetierkunde*, 53, 11–21

Hillibrand, M. (1974) *Analysis of Vertebrate Structure*, John Wiley and Sons, New York

Hisaw, F.L. (1923) 'Observations on the burrowing habits of moles (*Scalopus aquaticus machrinoides*)', *J. Mammal.*, 4, 79–88

Jelkmann, W., Oberthuer, W., Kleinschmidt, T. & Braunitzer, G. (1981) 'Adaptation of hemoglobin function to subterranean life in the mole *Talpa europaea*', *Respir. Physiol.*, 46, 7–16

Jensen, I.M. (1983) 'Metabolic rates of the hairy-tailed mole *Parascalops breweri* (Bachman, 1842)', *J. Mammal.*, 64, 453–462

—— (1986) 'Foraging strategies of the mole (*Parascalops breweri* Bachman, 1842), I. The distribution of prey', *Can. J. Zool.*, 64, 1727–1733, 'II. The economics of finding prey', *Can. J. Zool.*, 64, 1734–1738

Johannesan-Gross, C. von (1988) 'Lernversuche in einer Zweifachwahlapparatur zum Hell-Dunkel-Sehen des Maulwurfs (*Talpa europaea* L.)', *Z. Saugetierkunde*, 53, 193–201

Jones, J.K., Jr., Carter, D.C., Genoways, H.H., Hoffman, R.S., Rice, D.W., & Jones, C. (1986), 'Revised checklist of North American mammals north of Mexico', *Occas. Papers Mus., Texas Tech. Univ.*, 107, 1–22

Kirikov, S.V. (1946) 'On the periodic destruction of animals in the Southern Urals during severe winters with little snow', *Zool. Zh.*, 25, 565–570

Klevezal, G.A. & Kleinenberg, S.E. (1967) 'Age determination of mammals by layered

132

structure in teeth and bone', translation by the Translation Bureau, Foreign Languages Division, Department of the Secretary of State of Canada, 1969

Korn, H. (1986) 'A case of daily torpor in the golden mole *Amblysomus hottentotus* (Insectivora) from the Transvaal highveld, South Africa', *Saugetierkdl. Mitt.*, 33, 86–87

Krazovski, V.P. (1954) 'Nabljudenija za razmnozeniem vychucholi v uslovijach vol'ernogo soderzanija', *Zool. Zurn.*, 33, H. 1

Kuyper, M.A. (1985) 'The ecology of the golden mole *Amblysomus hottentotus*', *Mammal Rev.*, 15, 3–11

Larkin, P.A. (1948) 'Ecology of mole (*Talpa europaea* L.) populations', D.Phil. thesis, University of Oxford

Lichatschew, G.J. (1950) 'Uber der Einfluss des tiefgehenden Frostes in Walde auf den Maulwurfsbestand', *Bull. Soc. Nat. Moscou Biol.*, 55, 21–24

Ljungstrom, P.O. & Reinecke, A.J. (1969) 'Ecology and natural history of the microchaetid earthworms of South Africa. 4. Studies on influence of earthworms upon the soil and the parasitological question', *Pedobiologia*, 9, 152–157

Lodal, J. & Grue, H. (1985) 'Age determination and age distribution in populations of moles (*Talpa europaea*) in Denmark', *Acta Zool. Fennica*, 173, 279–281

Lyster, I.J.H. (1972) 'Mole kills Herring Gull', *Scottish Birds*, 7, 207–208

Macfadyen, A. (1963) 'The contribution of the soil fauna to total soil metabolism', J. Doeksen & J. van der Drift (eds.), *Soil Organisms*, North Holland Publishing Company, Amsterdam

Maser, C., Mate, B.R., Franklin, J.F., Dyrness, C.T. (1981), 'The natural history of Oregon coast mammals', *The US Dept. Agric. Forest Serv. Rept.* PNW-133: 1–496

Matthews, L. Harrison (1935) 'The oestrous cycle and intersexuality in the female mole (*Talpa europaea* Linn.)' *Proc. Zool. Soc. Lond.*, 347–383

Maynard Smith, J. (1982) *Evolution and the Theory of Games*, Cambridge University Press, Cambridge

Mellanby, K. (1966) 'Mole activity in woodlands, fens and other habitats', *J. Zool., Lond.*, 149, 35–41

—— (1967) 'Food and activity in the mole *Talpa europaea*', *Nature, Lond.*, 215, 1128–1130

—— (1971) *The Mole*, Collins, London

Milyutin, N.G. (1941) 'A note on the reproduction of the mole (*Talpa europaea brauneri* Satun)', *Zool. Zh.*, 20, 482–484

Morris, P. (1961) 'Some observations on the breeding season of the hedgehog and the rearing and handling of the young', *Proc. Zool. Soc. Lond.*, 136, 201–206

Morris, P. (1966) 'The mole as a surface dweller', *J. Zool., Lond.*, 149, 46–49

Ognev, S.I. (1928) *The Mammals of Eastern Europe and Northern Asia, Volume 1: Insectivora and Chiroptera*, Moscow and Leningrad, Translated from the Russian by the Israel Program for Scientific Translations, Jerusalem, 1962

Oppermann, J. (1968) 'Die Nahrung des Maulwurfs (*Talpa europaea L., 1758*) in unterschiedlichen Lebensraumen', *Pedobiologia* 8, 59–74

Peters, R.H. (1983) *The Ecological Implications of Body Size*, Cambridge University Press, Cambridge

Peterson, K.E. & Yates, T.L. (1980) '*Condylura cristata*', *Mammalian Species*, 129, 1–4, American Society of Mammalogists

Poduschka, W. & Richard, B. (1986) 'The Pyrenean desman — an endangered insectivore', *Oryx*, 20, 230–232

Puttick, G.M. & Jarvis, J.U.M. (1977) 'The functional anatomy of the neck and forelimbs of the Cape golden mole, *Chrysochloris asiatica* (Liptotyphla: Chrysochloridae)', *Zoologica Africana*, 12, 445–458

Quilliam, T.A. (1966) 'The mole's sensory apparatus', *J. Zool., Lond.*, 149, 76–78

Racey, P.A. (1978) 'Seasonal changes in testosterone levels and androgen dependent organs in male moles (*Talpa europaea*)', *J. Reprod. Fert.*, 52, 195–200

Redfern, R. & Mitchell, W. (1987) 'Successful keeping of the European mole (*Talpa europaea*) in captivity', *J. Zool., Lond.*, 212, 369–373

Reed, C.A. (1951) 'Locomotion and appendicular anatomy in three soricoid insectivores', *Am. Midl. Nat.*, 45, 513–671

Richard, P.B. (1976) 'Extension en France du Desman des Pyrenees et son environment', *Bull. Ecol.*, 7, 327–334

—— (1982) 'La sensibilité tactile de contact chez le desman (*Galemys pyrenaicus*)', *Biology of Behaviour*, 7, 325–336

—— (1985) 'Preadaptation of a Talpidae, the desman of the Pyrenees *Galemys pyrenaicus*,

G. 1811, to semi-aquatic life', *Z. Angew Zool.*, 72, 11–24

Roberts, A. (1951) *The Mammals of South Africa*, Central News Agency, Capetown

Satchell, J.E. (ed.) (1983) *Earthworm Ecology from Darwin to Vermiculture*, Chapman and Hall, London

Savage, R.J.G. & Long, M.R. (1986) *Mammal Evolution: An Illustrated Guide*, British Museum (Natural History), London

Schaefer, V.H. & Sadleir, R.M.F.S. (1979) 'Concentrations of carbon dioxide and oxygen in mole tunnels', *Acta theriol.*, 24, 267–276

—— (1981) 'Factors influencing molehill construction by the coast mole *Scapanus orarius*', *Mammalia*, 45, 31–37

Schaerffenberg, B. (1940) 'Die Nahrung des Maulwurfs (*Talpa europaea* L.)', *Z. Angew. Ent.*, 27, 1–70

—— (1941) 'Zur Biologie des Maulwurfs (*Talpa europaea* L.)', *Z. Saugetierkunde*, 14, 272–277

Scheffer, T.H. (1913) 'The common mole. Runway studies; hours of activity', *Trans. Kans. Acad. Sci.*, 25, 160–163

Skoczen, S. (1958) 'Tunnel digging by the mole (*T. europaea* Linne)', *Acta theriol.*, 2, 235–249

—— (1961) 'On food storage of the mole (*Talpa europaea* Linnaeus, 1758)', *Acta theriol.*, 5, 23–43

—— (1962) 'Age structure of the mole *Talpa europaea* Linnaeus 1758, from the food of the buzzard (*Buteo buteo* L.)', *Acta theriol.*, 6, 1–9

—— (1966) 'Stomach contents of the mole, *Talpa europaea* Linnaeus 1758, from Southern Poland', *Acta theriol.*, 11, 551–557

Smithers, R.H.N. (1983) *The Mammals of the Southern African Subregion*, University of Pretoria, Pretoria

Southern, H.N. (1954) 'Tawny owls and their prey', *Ibis*, 96, 384–410

Stein, G.H.W. (1950) 'Zur Biologie des Maulwurfs, *Talpa europaea* L.', *Bonn. Zool. Beitre.*, 1, 97–116

—— (1953) 'Uber Umweltabhangigkeiten bei der Vermehrung der Feldmaus, *Microtus arvalis*', *Zool. Jb. (Syst)*, 81, 527–547

Stoddart, D.M. (1976) 'Effect of the odour of weasels (*Mustela nivalis* L.) on trapped samples of their prey', *Oecologia*, 22, 439–441

Stone, R.D. (1985) 'Home range movements of the Pyrenean desman (*Galemys pyrenaicus*) (Insectivora: Talpidae)', *Z. Angew. Zool.*, 72, 25–36

Stone, R.D. & Gorman, M.L. (1985) 'Social organisation of the European mole (*Talpa europaea*) and the Pyrenean desman (*Galemys pyrenaicus*)', *Mammal Rev.*, 15, 35–42

Sullivan, T.P. & Crump, D.R. (1984) 'Influence of mustelid scent-gland compounds on suppression of feeding by snowshoe hares (*Lepus americanus*)', *J. Chem. Ecol.*, 10, 1809–1821

Swanton, E.W. (1938) *Country Notes and Nature Calendar*, E.W. Langham, Hazelmere and Farnham

Verner, J. (1977) 'On the adaptive significance of territoriality', *Am. Nat.*, 111, 769–773

Vleck, D. (1979) 'The energy cost of burrowing by the pocket gopher *Thomomys bottae*', *Physiol. Zool.*, 52, 122–136

—— (1981) 'Burrow structure and foraging costs in the fossorial rodent, *Thomomys bottae*', *Oecologia*, 49, 391–396

Vleck, D. & Kenagy, G.J. (unpublished) 'Digging performance of fossorial mammals: energetic significance of alternative morphologies'

Woods, J.A. & Mead-Briggs, A.R. (1978) 'The daily cycle of activity in the mole (*Talpa europaea*) and its seasonal changes, as revealed by radioactive monitoring of the nest', *J. Zool., London.*,184, 563–572

Yalden, D.W. (1966) 'The anatomy of mole locomotion', *J. Zool., Lond.*, 149, 55–64

Yates, T. (1983) 'The mole that keeps its nose clean', *Natural History*, 11/83, 55–60

Yates, T.L. & Greenbaum, I.F. (1982) 'Biochemical systematics of North American moles (Insectivora: Talpidae)', *J. Mammal.*, 63, 368–374

Yates, T.L. & Pedersen, R.J. (1982) 'Moles' in Chapman & Feldhamer (eds.), *Wild Mammals of North America: Biology, Management and Economics*, Johns Hopkins University Press, Baltimore

Yates, T.L. & Schmidly, D.L. (1978) '*Scalopus aquaticus*', *Mammalian Species*, 105, 1–4, American Society of Mammalogists

Yates, T.L., Pence, D.B. & Launchbaugh, G.K. (1979) 'Ectoparasites from seven species of North American moles (Insectivora: Talpidae)', *J. Med. Entomol.*, 16, 166–168

Index

scent marking 120–1
social behaviour 120–3
diet
methods of describing
39–40
of golden moles 40
of moles 40–2
of desmans 117–19
digging
amount of time spent
78–9
economics of 31
of eastern American
mole 17
of European mole 17–20
of Hottentot mole 17
of Namib mole 15–17
muscles used in 22–5
seasonal differences in
78–9
2,2-dimethylthietane
as a mole repellent
109–12
dinosaurs 1
adaptive radiation of 1
demise of 2
dispersal
mortality during 63–5,
120
timing 63, 120
distances travelled 78–80
distribution
of desmans 8, 113–14
of golden moles 5, 6
of shrews-moles, moles
and desmans 5, 8,
13–14

ears 47
earthworks 15–22
earthworms
biomass in soil 42
caches of 21
energy value 44
giant 40
in the diet of moles 40–4
water content 60
ectoparasites 128–9
Eimer's organs 9, 47–51
emigration 63–5
energy
costs of digging 26–32
costs of locomotion 26–8
costs of
thermoregulation
36–7, 53
value of earthworms 36
value of fat 35
epididymes
seasonal changes 58–9
evolution
of golden moles 7

of the mole humerus 26
of mammals 1–3
eyes
acuity 55–6
of golden moles 7
sensitivity to light 55

fat stores
size, in moles 35–6
energy content 35
fleas 128–9
flooding 20, 33
impact on desmans
116–17
food
availability for moles 68
caches of earthworms
21–2
daily intake by
moles 43–4
of desmans 117–19
seasonal changes in
intake by moles 45
foraging
in desmans 117–19
in golden moles 40
in moles 46–53
different strategies 51–3
fortress
cost of construction 34–5
food stores 21, 35–6
function 33–7
insulation value 36–7
method of construction
34–5
size 20
structure 20–1
where found 20, 33
fossils
of desmans 113
of golden moles 6
of moles and desmans 8
fur
evolution of 3
of desmans 115, 124
of golden moles 6–7
of moles 10
fur trade
impact on populations of
moles 72–4
in desmans 124–5

gestation
length of 61, 120
golden moles 4
adaptations for
digging 7
diet 40
distribution 5–6
eyes 7
fossil record 6
habitats 7

nest chamber 17
gonads 57–61
Greenland 5
growth
of young 62

habitat
territory size in
different 92–3
preference of
desmans 113–14
haemoglobin
adaptations for low
oxygen levels 32–3
in llamas 33
in moles 32
Hampton Court 15
heat 60–1, see also rut
hedgehogs 24
Hispaniola 5
home range, see also
territory
definition 88–9
of desmans 120–2
of moles 89–94
humerus
adaptations for digging
23–6
evolution 26
of moles 10
hyenas, spotted 57

identification textbooks 12
insectivora
ancestors and origin 4
characteristics of 2–4
dentition 3–4
diet 3
families of 4–5

Jacobite toast 15

King William III 15

lactation
duration 62, 120
energetic costs 54, 79
Life cycles
of moles 53
of desmans 120–2
lifespan 69–70, 120
life tables 69–70
limbs
adaptations for applying
force 22–6
as levers 22–3
litter size 61, 120–1
longevity 69–70, 120

Madagascar 5
mammals